Acknowledgements

My earnest thanks to my son, Jesse, for his work in the layout and graphic design of the cover of this book.

I would like to express sincere appreciation and thanks to Kelly Fuller, Pastor Dave Sczepanski, Pastor Darrell Arneson, Marsha Weber, Don Rogers, Pastor Mike O'Brien, Pastor Larry Dill, Kent Mabon, my brother and Jeri Mabon, my mother for all giving various types and degrees of input, help or encouragement, all of which assisted in the completion of this book. Thank you.

A special thanks for the many hours of detailed editing and red ink supplied by these friends: Bill and Irene Bennett, Anne Lively, Sharon Halvorsen and Pastor Max Doner. Their help was invaluable. Thank you very much.

And a special thanks to my good friend Scott Lively for his excellent chapter entitled *Christian Presuppositions of "Secular" Government*, Appendix A, at the close of this book. It is a needed and worthy perspective to the concepts set forth in the following pages.

Above all, my heartfelt thanks and love goes to my wife, Bonnie, who put numerous hours into the editing and completion of this effort. This book is as much hers as it is mine. Thank you, Baba!

Contents

Introduction

Chapter 1	— God Rules	1
Chapter 2	— God's Sovereignty in Action	19
Chapter 3	— God Owns Civil Government	45
Chapter 4	— The Prophet — John the Baptist	57
Chapter 5	— The Sword of the Lord	73
Chapter 6	— It's a Matter of Authority — Jurisdiction — Sovereignty	105
Chapter 7	— The Wall	123
Chapter 8	— Matters of a Practical Nature	135
Chapter 9	— The Goodness and Severity of God	157
Appendix A	— Christian Presuppositions of "Secular" Government by Scott Lively	169
Appendix B	— Organizations Active on Moral Issues	195
Footnotes		201

Introduction

When I realized that God had called me for an unknown time period to serve Him in the political realm, I proceeded as anyone would who was attempting to please Him and do His will. By grace I pursued it with all my might. In my heart I believed all that was needed was for somebody to step out and set an example. The folks who still believed in right and wrong from God's perspective would rally to the standard. We would arrest the moral decay, and head the culture back in the right direction. That was probably the most naive assumption I have ever made.

It wasn't long before I realized that the willingness of our society to allow the killing of preborn human beings by the millions indicated the existence of some deep-seated, severe problems. Hundreds of thousands of God's people barely utter a word in protest, let alone lift a finger of protection for God's creation, His little ones in the womb. Similarly, most of God's people do not believe that the fight to stop the homosexual agenda warrants their involvement, even though the sin of homosexuality is presented as an acceptable moral sexual expression to toddlers, children and older students in our public classrooms all across America.

Yet God Himself is both deeply concerned and involved. Unrestrained sin like abortion, homosexuality, pornography, and physician-assisted suicide cause God's involvement to shift from that of bringing conviction upon the specific individuals who practice such things to the bringing of corporate judgment upon the whole community.

The reason that the entire community suffers God's wrath is seen in Matthew 5:13 which says, "[I]f the salt loses its flavor, how shall it be seasoned? *It is then good for nothing but to be thrown out and trampled underfoot of man.*" A primary function of divine salt is to restrain moral decay in the larger community. If this is so, then the empirical evidence dictates the conclusion that the salt, at this time in history and in full view of Him who sits on the Throne, has lost its ability to season. Not only has the seasoning ability been lost, but this condition of apathy seems to be both desired and willful in the Church. There are many who go so far as to actually preach non-involvement — as if what goes on in the culture is none of God's concern. Subsequently the degree of apathy produced in many Christians, if not most, is staggering. The antithesis of apathy is the application of divine salt and light. We cannot be obedient to God and also be apathetic. The only way a Christian can walk in apathy is to be disobedient to God's will; therefore, apathy is sin. With this being the condition of the Church, is it any wonder that our culture has lost most of its moral restraint?

In the process of serving God in the political realm, I unexpectedly ran headlong into this anti-involvement, apathetic attitude. It was so pervasive in the Church that it forced me to go back to God and the Scriptures to find the biblical support for the call and burden He had placed in my heart, a burden which I believe is for every person who desires to be obedient to God, which is to be active in the political realm.

What you will read in the following pages is the truth of God as He has revealed it to me from His Word. This is not an exhaustive theological study on the subject, but simply an attempt to share with you what He showed to me. As the noble Bereans did, you must judge for yourself. I submit these pages to your conscience and to the Holy Spirit Who was sent to guide you into all truth. I only ask that you finish the book before you finalize your opinion. I am confident that the same Spirit who revealed these truths to me will also reveal them to you. When that occurs, please make haste to the battlefield — for much hangs in the balance.

Lon T. Mabon

Chapter 1

God Rules

At the outset, I want to submit to you two main propositions: First of all, God is sovereign. This is an absolute truth. He is the source and maintainer of all that exists. Therefore government, along with its functions, is undeniably an arena or institution created and maintained by Him.

And secondly, God is politically involved. To hold to any other notion is to not comprehend God's sovereignty over all things. He desires, in fact requires, that His people also be involved with Him in the political arena.

In the pages of this book, my objective is to prove that these statements are Biblically based, using the same sequence of scriptures God used when He revealed them to me. As I sought God for His truth concerning this much misunderstood arena, He showed me an aspect of Christianity that has been almost completely ignored or overlooked by the Church of our day.

I claim no special revelation, for others have seen these truths and spoken about them throughout the history of the Church. I was simply unaware of them, and the implications of many of the scriptures that I am about to present to you, until God revealed them to me by His Spirit. What I share with you in the following pages is entirely what God showed me when I inquired of Him regarding these matters.

The premise of this teaching is seen in one of the encounters God had with the Babylonian Empire, as recorded in Daniel 4. King Nebuchadnezzar ruled Babylon at the height of her power and influence, and it was this King whom God used to bring judgment upon a wayward Israel. God's dealings with King Nebuchadnezzar give us the elementary truths that provide the basis for the statements which open this chapter. The implications of God's use of a heathen king to bring judgment to His people will be fully discussed in this chapter and the next.

Judgment on a national scale is an option that God will exercise at His discretion when a society continues to ignore His moral requirements.

The Almighty used Babylon to bring judgment upon the people of Israel because they disregarded His ways. Though Israel and Judah had been warned by several prophets, they did not repent, and judgment came. Israel was conquered by Assyria. Later Judah was conquered by Babylon, which then also conquered Assyria.

In the second year of Nebuchadnezzar's reign, the king had a dream by which his spirit was disturbed and he could not sleep. Daniel, chapter four, states that this dream greatly troubled Nebuchadnezzar and made him afraid. He was not ignorant of the source of this dream, since he had been visited before in this manner by the God of Daniel. This king had experienced God's hand in times past, when not long before, he had seen a different vision while looking into a fiery furnace. Therefore, he would not take this new experience lightly.

Immediately upon waking, as if to prove a point, the king summoned his scribes to write a decree giving honor to the Most High God. He then called for all the wise men, magicians, astrologers, Chaldeans and soothsayers to assemble in the throne room and interpret his dream.

Keep in mind, King Nebuchadnezzar was not Jewish, but Babylonian. He was not part of the covenant, the promises, or the commonwealth of Israel. In fact, he was a heathen as it relates to the governmental and relational plans of God. This was not a theocracy, but a secular government, just as ours is. The comparison is exact.

The fundamental questions are: *Did God have the right to use Babylon and were King Nebuchadnezzar and Babylon under God's authority?*

It is the premise of this book that — YES — God could use Babylon. In fact, He could use anyone or anything, and — YES — absolutely everything is answerable to God's authority.

Although the Babylonians were making day-to-day choices contrary to God's moral requirements, nevertheless, they were not outside of God's universal and ultimate sovereignty over all things. Nor is any other living thing outside this sovereignty, whether it be an individual or the mightiest nation on the face of the earth. King Nebuchadnezzar, the king of Babylon, was, indeed, under God's authority whether he recognized it or not, or whether he acted like it or not, because God — the One True God — is sovereign over everything.

With the dream, God was exercising His authority over the king of Babylon. The servants of other gods and philosophies could not interpret the dream of the Almighty. Daniel, a servant of the Most High, was brought before the king. King Nebuchadnezzar was convinced that the "Spirit of the Holy God" was in Daniel, and would enable him to correctly interpret the vision.

Imagine the scene. All the *wise men* in the palace failed the king's command to interpret the dream. They were obviously apprehensive. Then came Daniel, standing in the most powerful place in the kingdom, talking to the most powerful man in the kingdom. The eyes of all the rulers and religious people of this kingdom were on Daniel, knowing that they had been unsuccessful in the same situation. This king exercised great authority. By his word people died immediately — no trial, no jury, just instantaneous, arbitrary judgment. In Daniel 4:10-16, as Daniel stood before him, the king spoke:

> These were the visions of my head while on my bed: I was looking, and behold, a tree in the midst of the earth, and its height was great. The tree grew and became strong; its height reached to the heavens, and it could be seen to the ends of all the earth. Its leaves were lovely, its fruit abundant, and in it was food for all. The beasts of the field found shade under it, the birds of the heavens dwelt in its branches, and all flesh was fed from it. I saw in the visions of my head while on my bed, and there was a watcher, a holy one, coming down from heaven.

> He cried aloud and said thus: "Chop down the tree and cut off its branches, strip off its leaves and scatter its fruit. Let the beasts get out from under it, and the birds from its branches. Nevertheless leave the stump and roots in the earth, bound with a band of iron and bronze, in the tender grass of the field. Let it be wet with the dew of heaven, and let him graze with the beasts on the grass of the earth. Let his heart be changed from that of a man, let him be given the heart of an beast, and let seven times pass over him."

Daniel explained the dream in verses 19 through 23. The main theme of the vision was the magnitude and scope of King Nebuchadnezzar's domain (symbolized by the grandeur of this huge tree). God's principle purpose in giving the vision was to reveal to King Nebuchadnezzar that the power and splendor of Babylon was not by man's hand, but by God's. *God Himself* reveals and establishes the baseline premise for the theme of this book when He demands that King Nebuchadnezzar understand and submit to a principle of the Kingdom of Heaven. The key Scripture is verse 17.

> This decision is by decree of the watchers, and the sentence by the word of the holy ones, in order that the living may know that *the Most High rules in the kingdom of men*, gives it to whomever He will, and sets over it the lowest of men.

Remember again to whom the Almighty was speaking. King Nebuchadnezzar was a pagan king. The Kingdom was heathenistic Babylon. God was informing King Nebuchadnezzar, in no uncertain terms, that He rules over every king, kingdom, domain, people, nation and every tongue — including Babylon.

The God whom Daniel worshiped rules over and within all the affairs and governmental activities of mankind. He always has and He always will. This includes all nations, governments and their leaders. He rules over everything.

God's decree was simple: If the king did not recognize God's divine authority over Babylon and himself, God's judgment would come upon him until he acknowledged that it is God who rules in the kingdoms of men. In verse 25, God told the king that he would suffer *"till* ... [he acknowledged] that the Most High rules in the kingdom of men, and gives it to whomever He chooses." In verse 26, Daniel said to the king: "your kingdom shall be assured to you, *after* you come to know that Heaven rules."

This is an extremely important principle, and it is critical that we learn to understand and apply it in our daily lives. For it can only be one of two ways. Either God rules the political affairs of nations, or the opposite is true — that the political affairs of men mean nothing to Him, in which case, our critics would have justification for their doctrine which advocates noninvolvement. But here, with Nebuchadnezzar, God did involve Himself and He involved His servant Daniel. It is undeniable that Daniel was placed before King Nebuchadnezzar to carry out the plan and will of God at this time and place in history. Daniel even gave counsel to the king himself, admonishing this pagan king on moral grounds when he said "break off your sins by being righteous" (Verse 27).

The man of God, acting in harmony with and obedience to His God, brought governmental authority into its rightful place of being subject to the moral claims of a Holy God.

God openly and clearly stated that He rules *"in* the kingdom of men." There is nothing in all of existence over which God does not have dominion. To emphasize this truth, He laid the godly requirement on this heathen Babylonian king to walk humbly, in recognition that the source of the authority and splendor of his domain was from God, not from King Nebuchadnezzar's hand. If the king refused to acknowledge this reality and instead exalted himself, taking the glory and credit, God would withdraw the human ability of understanding from the king; for seven years he would be like the beasts of the field.

It happened to King Nebuchadnezzar as Daniel said. We read in verses 29 through 32:

> At the end of the twelve months he was walking

about the royal palace of Babylon. The king spoke, saying, "Is not this great Babylon, that I have built for a royal dwelling by my mighty power and for the honor of my majesty?" While the word was still in the king's mouth, a voice fell from heaven: "King Nebuchadnezzar, to you it is spoken: the kingdom has departed from you! And they shall drive you from men, and your dwelling shall be with the beasts of the field. They shall make you eat grass like oxen; and seven times shall pass over you, until you know that the Most High *rules* in the kingdom of men, and gives it to whomever He chooses."

The word "rule" here in the Hebrew is "sholat," meaning "to have power, authority"[1] and "to rule, to have dominion."[2] One commentator says that "[t]he divine messenger concludes this announcement with the words that the matter was unchangeably decreed, for this purpose, that men might be led to recognize the supremacy of the Most High over the kings of the earth."[3] Another renders the key phrase of verse 17 this way: "that the living may know that the Lord is Most High over the kingdoms of men," and renders verse 25 as: "that the Most High is Lord of the kingdoms of men...."[4]

There is no doubt that the governments of men are under God's dominion. Here we see both God and Daniel involved in the ongoing affairs of government, rather than being separate from government.

The punishment on King Nebuchadnezzar was for the length of seven times. (Most scholars believe "a time" equals one year.[5]) That is a hard lesson. We should also recognize it as a very important lesson. Remember, verse 17 said that the sentence was given "in order that *the living* may know that the Most High rules in the kingdom of men..." Considering that the Holy Spirit ordained The Book of Daniel to be Holy Scripture for us today (see II Timothy 3:16), we must acknowledge that the substance of this lesson applies to *the living* of our day as well, in order that we also may know that the One True God exercises authority in and over the governments of men.

To his credit, King Nebuchadnezzar humbled himself (verses 34-35), but only after he learned the lesson the hard way. We read,

> And at the end of the time I, Nebuchadnezzar, lifted my eyes to heaven, and my understanding returned to me; and I blessed the Most High and praised and honored Him who lives forever: *For His dominion is an everlasting dominion, and His kingdom is from generation to generation. All* the inhabitants of the earth are reputed as nothing; He does according to His will in the Army of heaven *and among the inhabitants of the earth.* No one can restrain His hand or say to Him, "What have *You* done?"

God has authority over all the inhabitants of the earth. God has set up nations and He works within their governments. They exist by His authority. His will *shall* be performed. God can turn the hearts of powerful leaders. He can harden the heart (as with Pharaoh), humble the proud (as with Nebuchadnezzar), or give grace and favor to the godly (as with David). He does so *"in order that the living may know that the Most High rules in the affairs of men."* Psalm 22:27-28 supports this premise, saying,

> [a]ll the ends of the world shall remember and turn to the Lord, and all the families of the nations shall worship before You. For the kingdom is the Lord's, and *He rules over the nations.*

Psalm 33:10-15 also supports this:

> The Lord brings the counsel of the nations to nothing; He makes the plans of the peoples of no effect. The counsel of the Lord stands forever, the plans of His heart to all generations. Blessed is the nation whose God is the Lord, the people He has chosen as His own inheritance. The Lord looks from

heaven; He sees all the sons of men. From the place of His dwelling He looks on all the inhabitants of the earth; He fashions their hearts individually; He considers all their works.

The Lord God rules over everything — the individual, both saved and unsaved, families, peoples, governments and nations. Though some may choose to rebel against that truth, their action does not alter the reality that God still rules. God remains the Creator and the Almighty. If, in the providence of God, it does not happen in this life, there will, nevertheless, come a day in which everybody from the individual to the mightiest nation will come face to face with that reality. This life is but an opportunity in which we choose whom we are going to serve and, subsequently, how we want to spend eternity — an eternal existence with God or an eternal existence without God. With God we get all that He is. Without God we get all that He isn't.

We sometimes forget that in this life, God's influence is great upon the soul of the individual, as well as upon the culture. Romans 1:20 & 21 clearly states that God's invisible attributes, as well as His eternal power and divine nature, are visible and known to the human soul through that which is made, i.e., the creation. Matthew 5:45 says, "...He makes His sun rise on the evil and the good, and sends rain on the just and the unjust."

God's sovereignty and lordship are not contingent upon acknowledgment or recognition from those who serve themselves, and choose not to fear Him. Their rebellion does not alter the reality that *"the earth* is the Lord's and the fullness thereof," as recorded in I Corinthians 10:26 and Psalm 24:1. Some may never acknowledge the sovereignty of God, but that mere expression of ignorance does not, indeed cannot, affect in the slightest the fact that the will of God will prevail.

The Book of Daniel illustrates this. King Nebuchadnezzar thought that Babylon was a product of his own hand. For a long period in his life as king, he did not acknowledge or recognize the hand of God working in the kingdom of Babylon. The kingdom of Babylon was taken from King Nebuchadnezzar, but only for a period of time, until he learned the lesson. For the scripture says, Daniel told the King, "inasmuch as they gave the command to leave the stump and roots of the tree, your kingdom shall be assured to you, *after you come to know that heaven rules."* (Daniel 4:26). After Nebuchadnezzar's sanity returned, it was said that God's dominion, God's kingdom, and the will of God would prevail "among the inhabitants of the earth" (Daniel 4:34-35).

God created the physical realm. He works within the creation, moving it toward the purposes that He established within the counsel of His own will. Even with the free will of man factored in, and even with the principle of sin infecting human nature and the entire creation, God continues to work all things toward the completion of His will. We see this working in the way He used Babylon and Daniel, as well as in the way He dealt with the king.

Without question, there is a great mystery surrounding the sovereignty of God and the exercise of man's individual will. But it is also without question that both exist and work interconnectedly, yet independently. I am convinced that God does not make our choices for us in a way that overpowers our wills and is contrary to our own desires, but He does make us choose and He does, in a manner consistent with holiness, influence our choices. Even when He knows that once you choose, your choice will take you away from Him, He will set up circumstances where a choice must be made — but it will be your choice. God, as the Almighty, has the power and the right to present you with an option, the outcome of which He already knows. He cannot, because of who He is (morally pure by nature), make any person do wrong. It is not in Him to do so, nor to do any wrong. The possibility doesn't even exist. He cannot do wrong; therefore, He cannot make anyone do wrong. But if He knows a person's desire is to serve sin, not Him, He will force that person to make choices that lead either to repentance or to reprobation.

Reprobation is a spiritual condition in which God turns a person over to be dominated by the desired sin. However, that person is without excuse, because at the same time that God is giving him over to sin, that person is willfully choosing not to submit to His lordship, freely choosing sinful ways. If we choose our own way, ultimately, at the Judgment, God gives us the fulfillment of that choice, which is an eternal existence completely free of His moral influence and restraint. Through it all, in this physical life we remain God's creation. He made us. We exist because of Him. We continue to exist because He allows it, even down to the very air we breathe.

Sometimes we forget with whom we are dealing. Everything exists because God created it. Everything continues in existence because God keeps it going. Acts 17:23-28 proclaims this truth. The Holy Spirit says through the Apostle Paul:

> For as I was passing through and considering the objects of your worship, I even found an altar with this inscription: TO THE UNKNOWN GOD. Therefore, the One whom you worship without knowing, Him I proclaim to you: God, *who made the world and everything in it*, since He is Lord of heaven and earth, does not dwell in temples made with hands. Nor is He worshiped with men's hands, as though He needed anything, *since He gives to **all life, breath**, and **all things**. And He has made from one blood every nation of men to dwell on all the face of the earth and has determined their preappointed times and the boundaries of their dwellings*, so that they should seek the Lord, in the hope that they might grope for Him and find Him, though He is not far from each one of us; *for **in Him we live** and **move** and **have our being**....*

This is what the Church sometimes forgets. The sinner cannot sustain even his own existence without God. The very breath that the most cantankerous atheist breathes comes from God. When he shakes his fist at God, the very space he occupies and the movements he makes occur within God, *"for in Him we ... move...."* If we could remove all the molecules, atoms and smaller particles so there was no physical matter left, in the exact place where the matter was, would be God. He is even there at the same time the matter is, because He made and sustains the matter. This is one of the major attributes of Jehovah God — being omnipresent i.e., being in all places at the same time and being fully God. That is why the Apostle Paul says that even our moving about occurs in God. In the context of Acts 17, everything occurs in God; He knows all things in perfect detail. He knows even our innermost thoughts because our being, our existence, is in God. He knows the thoughts and intents of the heart because the heart exists in Him. He knows the deep recesses of each soul, areas of which some souls may not even yet be aware. Judgment day is going to be a simple matter for Him because He knows everything. In Him we live and move and have our being.

In Him, the nations also exist. All the governments of the world conduct their business within God. Each exists because of Him; civil government is an institution ordained by Him. Even if each government acts contrary to God's divine nature and will; each is, nevertheless, accountable to that nature and will.

God is God, whether a nation denies or upholds His authority and moral standard.

Every nation upon the face of the earth exists in God as the Holy Spirit defines in Acts 17:28. The Apostle states it in a created sense as well as an authoritative sense because all things are at all times accountable and answerable to God. God can, at any time, ask for an accounting. It is His right to do so and it will also be morally right, because He can do no wrong.

God is who He is and, ultimately, we will adjust and conform to Him, or we will give an account to Him as to why we have not. Then from a position of knowing all things, even the thoughts of our hearts, He will judge our actions and motives, whether we like it or not. It is not subject to our approval.

I want to clarify here that the Holy Spirit is definitely not teaching pantheism in Acts 17, nor am I. Pantheism teaches that there is no personal God. The god of pantheism is simply the sum total of all preexisting things. Whereas, I believe that the One True God created and sustains all things by His word and that He exists as the most supreme, perfect and personal Being throughout all eternity. We should not allow the fear of existing philosophies like pantheism, which distort the truth, to diminish our understanding of what the truth really is.

The key to Acts 17:28, is that these activities or conditions occur *"in Him,"* that is, they occur *in God Himself.* In context, the "in Him" is interpreted by verse 27. This whole passage of scripture is speaking to all human beings living in the creation saying, "so that they should seek the Lord, in the hope that they might grope for Him and find Him, *though He is not far from each one of us...*" Then verse 28 goes on in the same sentence saying, *"...for in Him we live and move and have our being..."* The context is the closeness of God. When we, as created human beings who live in Him, move in Him and have our very being in Him ask the question, "How close is He?" — we must answer as the Apostle does *"...not far from each one of us."* This is the context. For this is the same God presented in Romans 1:20, which says, "For since the creation of the world His invisible attributes *are clearly seen,* being understood *by the things that are made,* even His eternal power and Godhead, so that they are without excuse...." This is not pantheism; this is truth.

The pagan belief of pantheism teaches that the tree, the mountain and the stream, etc. are, collectively, god. But the Holy Spirit teaches that these things are the *creation* of the One True God, existing only by His spoken word. They do, nevertheless, reveal *clearly* His attributes, power and nature. All created things, including us, do exist in God Himself. I believe this is biblically-sound doctrine, yet, there are those who are so afraid of pagan philosophies (although we should be very cautious) that they go so far as to teach that the Apostle was not preaching truth here, but an accommodation, adjusting the truth of the gospel in order to reach the Greek philosophers. To me, that is a preposterous notion! For this is the same Apostle who wrote in Galations 1:6-12:

> I marvel that you are turning away so soon from Him who called you in the grace of Christ, to a different gospel, which is not another; but there are some who trouble you and want to pervert the gospel of Christ. But even if we, or an angel from heaven, preach any other gospel to you than what

we have preached to you, let him be accursed. As we have said before, so now I say again, if anyone preaches any other gospel to you than what you have received, then let him be accursed. For do I now persuade men, or God? Or do I seek to please men? For if I still pleased men, I would not be a bondservant of Christ. But I make known to you, brethren, that the gospel which was preached by me is not according to man. For I neither received it from man, nor was taught it, but it came through the revelation of Jesus Christ.

The message being delivered in Acts 17 was the gospel, for it convicted of sin (idolatry v.29), called for repentance (v.30), presented *"the Man"* and the resurrection (v.31), and led people to the Lord (v.34). And part of that message remains that *"...in Him we live and move and have our being."* For the One True God is all in all, and that includes the creation. It is God who rules and sustains the creation. Even if a segment of the creation rebels against Him, in order to accomplish His divine purposes, He may allow the creation to go on until His desires are fulfilled and His purposes completed.

Remember the parable of the tares in Matthew 13:24-30 where God let the good and bad seed grow up together until the time of the harvest. God will allow this present state of affairs to continue until the day of judgment, after which He will have a new creation wherein dwells righteousness (II Peter 3:13).

The working of His sovereign will within the creation — infested as it is with rebellion and sin and operating under the curse — is, indeed, a mystery. But the divine purpose of saving as many souls as possible from the eternal destruction of sin and rebellion weighs paramount on the heart of God. II Peter 3:9 says, "[t]he Lord is not slack concerning His promise, as some count slackness, but is *longsuffering* toward us, not willing that any should perish but that all should come to repentance."

If God, in his foreknowledge, knows which individuals are His, it stands to reason that He knows also which individuals will eternally choose sin to rule their lives. These individuals, by virtue of the choice made, are headed for eternal destruction (i.e., the ultimate fulfillment of their choice; to be free from any restraint by a moral God and to be separate from God and His goodness). Now if, along this path, God allows an option to come into their lives, knowing that they will act in a certain manner, and if they, by the exercise of their will, do act in that manner, and if that action causes another option whereby another individual chooses to give his life to God, and thus is saved from eternal destruction, is that a righteous course of events? Of course, it is! If He uses these *vessels of dishonor* (See Romans 9:21) to bring others to Himself, it is a righteous act. It is God's right to use those given over to sin for His glory, if He so chooses. Whatever He chooses to do will always be holy and good. He uses satan to advance His righteousness as well. He has done so in the past and He will do so again.

God may allow a nation to increase and prosper, even if it is a sinful nation, having arrived at that condition by the free exercise of the will of its citizens. He may then use that nation to accomplish His perfect purposes according to His will. If God so desires, He may step right into the middle of a nation at any given point in history, calling it to account because of the exceedingly sinful choices of its people (e.g., Sodom, Gomorrah, Nineveh and Babylon). He judged Sodom and Gomorrah because: **1)** He had a right to do so, and **2)** that act revealed for all generations His coming wrath against sin and also the coming day of judgment.

God uses individuals and nations to perform His will. God uses individuals and nations to establish His purposes. He will use everything and anything as He sees fit.

If, in all of this, a person attempts to find fault with God's management and maintenance of His creation, that faultfinding is based on ignorance produced by personal sin and rebellion. However, the sinful efforts to find fault with perfection do not alter that perfection in the slightest, nor do they deter God from using the creation or created individuals in a fashion that produces the optimum possibility that souls will accept His grace, or at least be presented with the most favorable opportunity for such acceptance.

God will also uphold His righteousness, at His discretion, in a visible manner and based on His judgment and wisdom. He will also make known the fact that His righteousness rules all of existence. That option is His. He is God. It is His right.

Part of acknowledging ultimate reality is comprehending the truth of God's absolute lordship over everything in existence and His right to rule. Opinions to the contrary do not run, affect, or alter the universe; in fact, the essence of that philosophy is the height of sinfulness. This is not to say we cannot or should not have questions. But when we begin questioning His sovereignty, however, with statements like "I cannot serve God or I cannot even believe in God because I would not do this or that this way or that way or I would do it another way," then without a shadow of doubt, the "I" has been exalted above God. That is the very core impulse and substance of sin. When challenging God's sovereignty becomes the heartfelt expression of an individual, know that sin is ruling in that life. But even if every soul were in that condition, it would not alter the truth that God is the source of all existence, that all existence is accountable to Him, and that He is holy.

It is my opinion that one of satan's primary claims before God is that, once freedom of choice is granted to a creature, that creature will desire to be independent from his source and that once becoming a living soul, that soul, as satan himself did, will act in a self-centered manner, rather than in a God-centered manner. But there are countless individuals who have chosen to give their souls back to God. Such individuals have acknowledged that when the soul rules itself, it is being ruled by sin, which begets further and continuous sin. Those individuals have also acknowledged the truth that only God, in and of Himself, can be and is holy.

God does not require our understanding in order to exercise His will, but from believers, He does require trust. God's judgment, His knowledge, His nature, His love and His heart can be trusted. As the struggle between right and wrong works itself out within the confines of the creation, what God does require is our belief that He is the Almighty and that, therefore, it is impossible for Him to do any wrong. There are a myriad of things that we don't understand, but do we understand that He is God Almighty? Do we understand that He is *perfect* and incapable of wrongdoing?

God rules in the affairs of men. What He does or doesn't do, what He allows or doesn't allow, is based upon His will, His purpose and His holy nature of love. He will use the nations as He sees fit. Furthermore, what He sees fit to do will always be holy and pure because of who He is. He allowed Babylon to rise in dominance, even though its soothsayers, astrologers and magicians acted in contradiction to His moral requirements. Each one chose to be so, and each one will give an accounting of what he did with the life God gave him. Yet at the same time God used each of them for His purposes, as He deemed appropriate. God has used the devil before and will use him over and over again when the end result advances righteousness. God will use all things to advance His will, knowing also that on the day God has set aside for judgment, each person will give an account of the choices that he has made. No one will escape the moral audit, nor will any single action, word or thought be ignored. All will be exposed, and in the meantime, God will use all things to advance His moral cause.

There is another principle at work here: *when good people lower their standards and refuse to do good and to require good in their culture, evil increases and becomes stronger. Evil only increases where those who should protect good fail to do so.* This principle will be addressed in later chapters in this book.

Israel was troubled by her neighbors when, as a nation, she allowed evil to establish itself and increase within her borders. God actually forces the issue. He works to "make the tree good, or make it evil."(It is an aspect of God's ongoing active judgment. When we walk in our own ways, we get what we deserve: we eat the fruit of our own ways (See Matthew 12:33). *The evil we allow becomes the source of our judgment. As a nation and culture, our failure to deal with sin, thus our tolerance of it, becomes the actual starting point for national judgment.*

As St. Thomas Aquinas observed:

> [F]or men to merit [good government] they must abstain from sinning, because it is as a punishment for sin that, by divine permission, the impious are allowed to rule....So guilt must first be expiated

before the affliction of tyranny can cease.

Only the power and will of God, working through His people, restrains evil in this world, but His commitment to use his power is tied to the self-will of man. When we choose evil over good, God allows evil to reign.

In summary, God is undeniably involved within the political structures of our nations, as He was in Babylon. Without question, God visited King Nebuchadnezzar in a dream so that people living *today* could know that *"the Most High rules in the affairs of men."*

With the Psalmist, in chapter 67, we can witness to this truth:

> God be merciful to us and bless us, and cause His face to shine upon us, Selah. That Your way may be known on earth, Your salvation among *all nations*. Let the peoples praise You, Oh God; let all the peoples praise You. Oh, *let the nations* be glad and sing for joy! For You shall judge the people righteously, and *govern the nations* on the earth. Selah. Let the peoples praise You, oh God; let all the peoples praise You. Then the earth shall yield her increase; God, our own God, shall bless us. God shall bless us, and all the ends of the earth shall fear Him.

And II Chronicles 20:6 asks this rhetorical question,

> O Lord God of our fathers, are You not God in heaven, and do You not *rule over all the kingdoms of the nations*, and in Your hand is there not power and might, so that no one is able to withstand You?

This is a fundamental concept in the kingdom of God. *"For God is the King of all the earth ... God reigns over the nations..."* (Psalm 47:7-8). It is an essential truth in the Christian faith. *THE MOST HIGH RULES IN THE AFFAIRS OF MEN.*

Chapter 2

God's Sovereignty in Action

The story of Joseph sold as a slave by his brothers to the Midianite traders marks the beginning of an important chain of events in the ongoing eternal plan of God. It reveals much to us concerning God's involvement in the political affairs of the nations.

God's plan led a young man, Joseph, to Potiphar's house. Something happened there which, on the surface, could be viewed as an unjust event, which resulted in Joseph's being thrown into prison (See Genesis 39). It was in this prison that he met the chief butler of Pharaoh's court. Because Joseph was able to interpret a dream given by God to the chief butler, he found himself standing before Pharaoh (at the butler's recommendation) to interpret another dream, one that Pharaoh had received from God. Pharaoh's dream involved seven fine and fat cows that ate seven inferior and gaunt ones, and also seven plump and good heads of grain that devoured seven thin heads. Joseph correctly interpreted the dream and Pharaoh's response was exactly what God wanted.

God set up this elaborate chain of events, which after the passage of several years, placed this young Hebrew man before Pharaoh of Egypt, gaining him favor with that heathen king. God elevated Joseph politically. This is evidenced by Pharaoh's words to Joseph in Genesis 41:40-44:

> You shall be *over* my house, and all my people shall be *ruled* according to your word; *only* in regard to the throne will I be greater than you. And Pharaoh said to Joseph: "See, I have set you over all the land of Egypt." Then Pharaoh took his signet ring off his hand and put it on Joseph's hand;

> and he clothed him in garments of fine linen and put a gold chain around his neck. And he had him ride in the second chariot which he had; and they cried out before him, "Bow the knee!" So he set him over all the land of Egypt. Pharaoh also said to Joseph, "I am Pharaoh, and *without your consent no man may lift his hand or foot in all the land of Egypt.*"

No one can question that this was governmental authority of the highest degree — and by God's hand, Pharaoh gave it to Joseph. *God is politically involved!*

Egyptian governmental authority was given to Joseph because of God's direct involvement. The task which Joseph faced was to prepare the whole country for the coming seven years of famine, as represented by the seven inferior cows and seven thin heads of grain in Pharaoh's dream. Joseph was, in essence, made *Vice Pharaoh* with specific responsibility to oversee Egypt's *Department of Agriculture*. The entire country was now placed under the authority of his decisions on agricultural policy. Genesis 41:47-49 reads:

> Now in the seven plentiful years the ground brought forth abundantly. So he gathered up all the food of the seven years which were in the land of Egypt, and laid up the food in the cities; he laid up in every city the food of the fields which surrounded them. Joseph gathered very much grain, as the sand of the sea until he stopped counting, for it was immeasurable.

Did God do this for the sake of Egypt? No. Egypt had long ago given itself up to the worship of demons (a choice made within the confines and the scope of the free will of man). Yet the people of Egypt also operated, albeit in ignorance, under the higher authority of the One True God. *God is capable of performing His will, yet leaving man with his own free will.* Remember that God, in His unique position of being God, knows all things. Every individual soul is created by God, and continues to exist with God as its source. There is no independent reality that exists apart from God. Hell is the only place that comes close to such a state. In hell, God purposes not to manifest any of His divine influence, attributes or presence. Yet, even without these expressions, the Scripture still says He is there. This is because the things that exist, even hell itself, do so only because God exists.

If all of existence were a painting, God would be the canvas, the paint and the brush, as well as the painter. The fact that He decided to take from Himself and give life to the images on the canvas, making living souls of them, does not alter the reality that He remains the canvas, the paint, the brushes and the painter. He has, as well, become the One who gave life to the images. Without Him there would be no existence. Without Him there would be no life. Therefore, self-reliance (and even rebellion against God) cannot attain a state of independence from God.

Choices made in opposition to God's moral will are made in defiance to God's authority. To their sorrow and anger, many people will some day find out that God is God, that He is existence itself, and that He is holy. At an appointed time in the future, everyone, having been given the ability of choice and action, must give an accounting of what he produced through the use of that gift. The standard for the accounting is God Himself; He is all that the word *God* implies in His relation to right and wrong, good and evil. As to His morality, He is pure, righteous and holy. He is morally perfect. God is also the very substance of existence; He will therefore forever be the standard by which, and to which, we must account.

Picture in your mind's eye two parallel, concurrent levels of the same reality. The lower level is the place where a multitude of living souls interact with each other as individuals, as families and as nations (governments), each one having a multitude of options, temptations and choices. As individuals, each of us is thinking his own thoughts, having his own desires — acting on some, rejecting others — sometimes deeply concerned about, and at other times oblivious to, the upper level. The upper level is the realm in which God is active in the "affairs of men" (Daniel 4:17), where God is painting on the canvas, unseen and yet evident to those who have eyes to see.

Egypt, moving along historically and making decisions on that lower level of reality, was nevertheless doing so on the canvas of God's existence. God was, at the same time, maintaining an ongoing eternal plan on that upper level of reality, a plan which was also being worked out in the physical realm.

We see this in that God was active in the "affairs of men" in Egypt. God was involved! God was involved politically when he placed Joseph within the Egyptian government so He could carry out His eternal purpose. God gave Pharaoh the dream. God guided circumstances to bring Joseph to Egypt, to Potiphar's house, into jail, into the life of Pharaoh's butler and ultimately into the presence of Pharaoh. God, using Pharaoh as His instrument, placed Joseph over Egypt. *God was involved in the politics of Egypt. So was His man, Joseph!*

When Joseph was offered the position by Pharaoh, he did not reply, "God does not want His people involved in politics; therefore, I must humbly decline!" He did not say, "My pastor said I should only be involved in prayer and in gaining converts to God's covenant of circumcision" (which was the covenant to which Joseph was submitted at the time — Genesis 17:1-14). No such notion existed then — and no such notion exists in the New Covenant.

Politics is the inner workings and the activities of government. God is involved and, like Joseph, so should His people be.

God's plan concerned his people, Israel, as the descendants of Abraham from whose lineage the Messiah would come, according to God's covenant with Abraham. Because of the coming seven year famine, God, in His foreknowledge, knew that Jacob and his sons could survive only in Egypt — and only if God caused Egypt to store up a seven years' supply of grain. But He had to arrange to get someone into Egypt to be promoted politically, someone who would have the motivation to save Jacob. Such a person would have to trust God completely of his own free will because God would not violate that person's free will. It would have to be someone who would surrender his will into God's hand — even to the point of enduring several years of personal hardships and crushing disappointments. In God's mind, Joseph was that man.

To fully understand the high degree of God's involvement, we must look deeper into the working of the free will of man and the sovereign will of God. We can gain that understanding by asking the question: *Do the following scriptures contradict each other?*

1. From the Lord's prayer directed to His Father, Matthew 6:13: "and do not lead us into temptation ..."
2. James 1:13: "Let no one say when he is tempted, 'I am tempted by God' for God cannot be tempted by evil, nor does He Himself tempt anyone."
3. Matthew 4:1: "Then Jesus was led up *by the Spirit* into the wilderness *to be tempted by* the devil."
4. Job 6:4: "...for the arrows of the Almighty are within me; My spirit drinks in their poison; The terrors of God are arrayed against me."
5. James 1:12: "Blessed is the man who endures temptation; for when he *has been approved,* he will receive the crown of life which the Lord has promised to those who love Him."

From these scriptures we can clearly ascertain that personal temptation will come, but when a person resists it, victory and a reward follow. They are not contradictory to each other. God allows, sometimes even orchestrates a circumstance in which temptation will occur, but He will never personally tempt. In fact, it is impossible for Him to tempt anyone to do evil because of who He is. The actual decision to do evil, therefore, must come from the individual, for it cannot come from God, nor can He influence someone to do evil. That also would be wrong, and He is incapable of doing wrong. But He can and will test us, and He will use the results of our own choices to advance what is right and good.

Keeping all this in mind, let us look at Genesis 45:1-4, where Joseph finally revealed his true identity to his brothers. Starting at the first verse, we read:

> Then Joseph could not restrain himself before all those who stood by him, and he cried out, "Make everyone go out from me!" So no one stood with him while Joseph made himself known to his brothers. And he wept aloud, and the Egyptians and the house of Pharaoh heard it. Then Joseph said to his brothers, "I am Joseph; does my father still live?" But his brothers could not answer him, for they were dismayed in his presence. And Joseph said to his brothers, "Please come near to me." So they came near. Then he said: "I am Joseph your brother, whom you sold into Egypt."

First of all, we notice that Joseph spoke, with reference to himself, saying "...*whom you* sold into Egypt." We remember this clearly from Genesis 37. They put him into the pit and then pulled him out to sell him to the Midianite traders. They knew what they had done, and now they were "dismayed in his presence." Verse five confirms this when Joseph says: "But now, do not therefore be grieved or angry *with yourselves* because *you sold me* here; *for **God sent me** before you to preserve life*" This scripture represents the two parallel realities, or planes of our existence: those actions which occur by the actual working of our free will, and the level of action that is being produced by God Himself, based on the counsel of His perfect and sovereign will.

Although it is true that God will not, in fact cannot, directly tempt anyone to do evil, as we read in Scripture, He can and does allow individuals to be tempted. In fact, dealing with temptation to do evil is part of the ongoing process leading to salvation, and then to sanctification. We saw that the Spirit *drove* Jesus (Mark 1:12) into the wilderness to be *tempted* (Matthew 4:1) by the devil for *forty days* (Luke 4:2). God can, does and will allow everyone to be tempted. In truth, He will (as with Job) help make the arrangements. As with Joseph, He will help set up the circumstances.

In this age, there are only three types of individuals: **1)** those who have given their lives to God completely, **2)** those who are moving toward or away from God, and **3)** those who have permanently rejected God. God will bring circumstances into the lives of the first group (1) so that they will overcome the inner sin we all have. Into the lives of the second group (2), God will bring circumstances that will allow them to prove what is in their hearts, determining which direction they will ultimately go. Into the lives of the third group (3), He will bring about circumstances to compel them to make free-will decisions, the results of which He will use to affect, in a positive manner, the other two. Those decisions are used to play an eternal role in His on-going plan. Such were the decisions of the Pharaoh who battled with Moses.

Keep in mind that God is the canvas. Thoughts, motivations, decisions, and actions are being played out on the canvas of God's own existence. He knows what is in every individual heart. Even though He knows all things, He has obligated Himself, nevertheless, to work within the limited realm where mankind resides. That is why both planes exist — the level of man's will and the level of God's sovereignty — both working within the creation. We see this demonstrated in the Garden of Eden after the fall of humanity, which is fully contained and represented in Adam and Eve. God called out to them, "Where are you?" In His omniscience, He knew where they were. He knows if a sparrow falls to the ground (Matthew 10:29) because He is the canvas upon which the creation exists. He knows the number of hairs on each person's head (Matthew 10:30), but He has obligated Himself to interact directly with man only within the realm in which man lives, and under the limitations He has placed on humanity. Yet at the same time, He knows all things and He is working on His own level, parallel to the level in which He is also directly interacting with mankind under mankind's inherent limitations.

Again, this is evident in His dealing with Joseph and his brothers, and then with Pharaoh. When we look at the outward situation, the betrayal of Joseph by his brothers seems a sinful act, motivated by jealousy and hatred. Indeed, it was all of that. But God, knowing the hearts of Joseph's brothers at that time, used their personal, willful choices to accomplish His higher purposes and goals. Remember, it was the dream Joseph had that revealed the brothers' sinful tendencies and precipitated their subsequent actions. Joseph told his dream to his father and brothers, indicating that they would one day bow down to him. Genesis 37:10-11 reads,

> So he told it to his father and his brothers; and his father rebuked him and said to him, "What is this dream that you have dreamed? Shall your mother and I and your brothers indeed come to bow down to the earth before you?" And his brothers *envied him*, but his father kept the matter in mind.

God knew beforehand what each of their reactions would be. God did not in any way force their will to cause them to sin. The Scripture is clear on that subject: *"Let no one say when he is tempted, 'I am tempted by God'; for God cannot be tempted by evil, nor does He Himself tempt any man."* (James 1:13)

Temptation is not external, but internal. That which is causing the temptation may be external, but the reason it is enticing a man is internal. That is why James continues in Verse 14, saying: "[b]ut each one is tempted when he is drawn away *by his own desires* and enticed. Then when desire is conceived, it gives birth to sin; and sin, when it is full-grown, brings forth death." And verses 16 and 17 go on to say: *"Do not be deceived,* my beloved brethren. Every good gift and every perfect gift is from above, and comes down from the Father of lights, with whom there is no variation or shadow of turning."

God cannot be tempted with evil. Why? Because there is nothing in God that would or could respond to evil. To be enticed is not sin; sin occurs only when you either think the enticement to completion ("...whoever *looks* at a woman *to lust* for her has already committed adultery with her in his heart...." Matthew 5:28), or you actually perform the deed, to which the desire led. An infraction can occur only when a person actually participates in the prohibited activity, whether in thought or deed. For instance, in the story of David and Bathsheba recorded in II Samuel 11, first David *saw*, then he *looked*, and then he *acted*. Sin, as a principle, exists in the human heart and spirit, within our nature, because of the fall of Adam and Eve. Sin continues to reside there because each individual consents to its mastery and lordship. The fact that sin resides in us is the overriding problem.

Though God cannot, and therefore does not, directly urge evildoing, in His sovereignty, He already knows what choice will be made or what action will be taken by an individual. He brings, or allows, a scenario in order to create the opportunity in which that person will exercise his free will, knowing that the chosen action will be exactly the one that He can use to advance righteousness and His perfect plan.

Consider again the two parallel levels of truth: **1)** God's perspective and His sovereign will in bringing or allowing the circumstance, and **2)** the concurrent perspective of free will, which recognizes that God does not directly cause an individual to make a certain choice, but that instead, a person voluntarily exercises his own will in response to the circumstance. The fact that both perspectives are true is an even greater testimony to the greatness of God. His will is going to be accomplished at the same time that man will stand before God on Judgment Day and give an account of his actions, produced by the working of his own voluntary will. It is a mystery, but the portion of it that we can understand is amazing!

Joseph's brothers reacted as God knew they would. He was planning on it. But did He manipulate them to respond in order to make His plan succeed? Did God's influence come upon them and force them, against their own wills, to do evil? NO, of course not. There is no such possibility in all of existence or throughout all of eternity.

The degree to which a person believes that God is holy, devoid of evil, is the degree to which he will believe that it is impossible for God to directly influence someone to do evil.

At the same time and on another level, He brought certain circumstances directly into the lives of Joseph's brothers, thereby setting up a situation in which they had to make a choice. This choice required them to exercise free will.

The degree to which a person believes that God is almighty and sovereign is the degree to which he will acknowledge God's right to act in a sovereign manner.

This fact is also very much a part of reality. Romans 9:18,

referring to God, says: "...He has mercy on whom He wills, and whom He wills He hardens." Does this scripture contradict James 1:13 ("let no one say when he is tempted, 'I am tempted by God'; for God cannot be tempted by evil, nor does He Himself tempt anyone.")? Does Romans 9:18, quoted above, contradict Romans 2:11 ("...there is no partiality with God.")? Of course not! For there are two concurrent levels, two separate and distinct perspectives, which are not in conflict.

Scripture uses both perspectives when referring to a later Pharaoh, the one who struggled with Moses. Exodus 4:21 says:

> And the Lord said to Moses, "When you go back to Egypt, see that you do all those wonders before Pharaoh which I have put in your hand. *But I will harden his heart*, so that he will not let the people go."

This is the divine perspective: God's direct intervention in Pharaoh's life, the result of which produced hardness in Pharaoh's heart. It cannot be denied, overlooked or diminished. God does take direct action in people's lives and in the affairs of nations. The results of His involvement, from a *human* perspective, are often viewed as negative. Even though the Scripture says that God hardened Pharaoh's heart, it also says in Exodus 8:15, "...when Pharaoh saw that there was relief, _he_ hardened _his_ heart and did not heed them, *as the Lord had said.*"

We look at the same situation from the perspective of the second level and it is just as real and valid as the first. It is man's free-will response to options and circumstances, even those situations allowed or directly brought by God into our lives by God.

It cannot be denied, overlooked or diminished. God allows us to be tempted, He may even directly lead us to a place of temptation (as He did with Jesus in Matthew 4:1), but He will never personally influence us to do wrong. NEVER! He cannot, for He is holy, and we thank Him that He is. Blessed be His name forever!

Exodus 10:1 says:

> Now the Lord said to Moses, "Go in to Pharaoh; for *I have hardened his heart* and the hearts of his servants, that I may show these signs of Mine before him...."

God knew *this* Pharaoh's heart just as He knew the heart of the previous Pharaoh, before whom He brought Joseph. He knew what each set of circumstances would produce within the heart of each Pharaoh. God knew beforehand just how each man would exercise his will in response to the situations He brought into his life. Pharaoh exercised his free will and was accountable to God for those real, voluntary actions. It is also correct, and should not be troubling to us, to say that God hardened Pharaoh's heart through the circumstances He brought into his life.

To some this duality represents a sticky theological problem. However, I maintain that Scripture teaches the absolute reality of this perspective of God's complex influence: God's actions in people's lives — even upon governments — produce results, some of which are apparently negative. But they only seem negative because of the exercise of the human will. The Apostle Paul also maintains this in Romans 9:19-23:

> You will say to me then, "Why does He still find fault? For who has resisted His will?" But, indeed, O man, *who are you to reply against God?* Will the thing formed say to him who formed it, "Why have you made me like this?" Does not the potter have power over the clay, from the same lump to make one vessel for honor and another for dishonor? What if God, wanting to show His wrath and to make His power known, *endured with much longsuffering* the vessels of wrath prepared for destruction, and that He might make known the riches of His glory on the vessels of mercy, which He had prepared beforehand for glory....

This inspired word is one hundred percent accurate, portraying the divine perspective perfectly. It reveals with overwhelming clarity God's direct involvement in each person's life. It states clearly that, just as a potter uses clay, He will use both the reprobates (*vessels of wrath* who have permanently set their hearts and minds to defy God) and also the *vessels of mercy* (those who, because of surrendering to God in the salvation of their souls, actually seek to do God's will). All of this is done without violating James 1:13, which says, "Let no one say when he is tempted, 'I am tempted by God'; for God cannot be tempted by evil, nor does He Himself tempt anyone," or Romans 2:11, which says, "For there is no partiality with God," or I Peter 1:17, which says: "...if you call on the Father, *who without partiality judges according to each one's **work***, conduct yourselves throughout the time of your stay here in fear ...."

The scripture that teaches God's direct involvement also teaches that His judgment is based on the choices made by each individual (*one's work*) and is determined without partiality. The only works God will judge will be those done by the individual himself, which are the result of choices made as circumstances have arisen.

Scripture clearly reveals that God does not will any person to do evil. If He did so, He would not be God. If He could do so, He would not be perfect, and therefore would not be God. It is foolishness even to entertain such a thought. Therefore, I believe the scripture teaches that God does not make *vessels of wrath* or *dishonor* by influencing individuals against their will to do evil. We can understand how human evil, nevertheless, fits into God's plan by envisioning two levels coexisting and operating at the same time — God's bringing or allowing circumstances to enter a person's life which create a set of options, and concurrently, the resultant decision and action being carried out by the exercise of the free will of the individual.

From the perspective of God's involvement, He knew that if He brought this chain of events into Pharaoh's life, Pharaoh would make a free-will decision, based on the evil in his heart, and that decision would be against God's people. As we read in Exodus 10:1, God said, "... for I have hardened his heart and the heart of his servants." Because of the circumstances God brought, as well as the knowledge God had of the evil condition of Pharaoh's heart, God knew

Pharaoh's decision would be to harden. Even though God neither overpowered Pharaoh's weak and resistant human will, nor by power of His superiority, forced Pharaoh to do evil, He nevertheless hardened Pharaoh's heart; he brought the circumstances that caused Pharaoh to voluntarily make the decision to do so. Therefore, from that perspective, God hardened his heart. But at the same time, with equal correctness and validity because the decision was made by Pharaoh alone and apart from a force that made him do wrong against his will, Scripture can equally say in Exodus 9:34, that "...when Pharaoh saw that the rain, the hail, and the thunder had ceased [i.e., the circumstances], he sinned yet more; [i.e., the evil in Pharaoh's heart] and *he* hardened *his* heart [i.e., the exercising of his free will], he and his servants."

God hardened Pharaoh's heart. Pharaoh hardened his own heart. Both statements, made from two very real and coexisting perspectives, are accurate and true. The same truths hold constant concerning Joseph's Pharaoh. God knew his heart and knew he would voluntarily act in the positive manner in which he did, given the nature of the dreams and the fact that the chief butler and Joseph were together in Pharaoh's jail.

The same truths are established in the story of Joseph and his brothers. Since God knew their hearts, He knew that they would voluntarily respond with envy and hatred toward Joseph, because of his dreams and the coat of many colors (Genesis 37:3). The brothers failed a moral test, but God used their failure to begin the necessary chain of events which led to the political promotion of Joseph to the position of Governor of all Egypt (Genesis 45:26).

Let no one doubt that it was personal, willful sin which Joseph's brothers plotted and carried out. Later in this part of God's plan for the ages, Joseph's father Jacob died. Scripture records this in Genesis 50:15-20:

> When Joseph's brothers saw that their father was dead, they said, "Perhaps Joseph will hate us, and may actually repay us for all *the evil which we did to him.*" So they sent messengers to Joseph, saying, "Before your father died he commanded, say-

ing, 'Thus you shall say to Joseph: I beg you, please forgive *the trespass* of your brothers and *their sin; for they did evil* to you. (Author's note: Only personal works are judged as trespasses and sins — only personal acts or thoughts produced by the voluntary exercise of one's will — and here the Scripture, inspired by the Holy Spirit, classifies their acts as sin.) Now, please, forgive the trespass of the servants of the God of your father.'" And Joseph wept when they spoke to him. Then his brothers also went and fell down before his face, and they said, "Behold, we are your servants." Joseph said to them, "Do not be afraid, *for am I in the place of God?* But as for you, <u>you meant</u> evil against me; but <u>God meant it for good</u>, in order to bring it about as it is this day, to save many people alive."

Notice the two dimensions of the term *"meant."* This is an *important* distinction, because it demonstrates the exercising of *two different wills*. It also clearly illustrates the two perspectives or levels. The first is the willful purpose of man, his works, his choices, his deeds — the history he makes on the canvas of God. They are the record made on the pages of reality and truth for which each man and nation will give an accounting. The second *"meant"* indicates the actions of God as the painter. God takes the individual choices painted on the canvas and utilizes them, causing or allowing circumstances to enter the current of recorded history of an individual life or nation. In this manner, he brings about further choices which "...either make the tree good and its fruit good, or else make the tree bad and its fruit bad; for a tree is known by its fruit." (Matthew 12:33) God hates lukewarmness. He would that we were either hot or cold. Anything else seems, figuratively, to make Him ill. In Revelation 3:15-16, He says, "I know your works, that you are neither cold nor hot. *I could wish you were cold or hot.* So then, because you are lukewarm, and neither cold nor hot, I will vomit you out of My mouth."

Scripture shows us the two levels of concurrent historical activity; both are valid, both are real, both exist. The reality and functioning of the one does not violate the other. We can clearly see them in the story of Joseph.

It cannot be denied that God was involved in the political affairs of Egypt, causing His man to be placed in a strategic position in the government of a pagan society, in order to advance His plan for the ages.

God did not teach or suggest then, nor does He teach or suggest today, that it is improper to be involved in the political affairs of governments, even pagan ones. Obviously, neither does He declare that it is improper for His people to be involved.

We witnessed God working within the government of Nebuchadnezzar, King of Babylon, and again with Pharaoh of Egypt — in a political context in both cases. We can see this in the story of yet another ancient ruler, King Ahasuerus of Persia.

Persia had defeated Babylon in battle and the Persian Empire ruled over much of the Middle East. The capital of this sprawling empire was Shushan where the king resided with Queen Vashti. In approximately 483 BC, when summoned by the King to a feast, Queen Vashti refused the king's command. This triggered a chain of events which again led to the saving of God's people. King Ahasuerus (Xerxes in Greek) decided to replace Queen Vashti with a new queen. When Mordecai (a high government official) heard of the plan he moved Esther, a young Jewish girl whom he had raised (his uncle's daughter) into a position from which, if she found favor, she could be chosen queen (Esther 2:7). In God's providence, Esther became queen of the Persian Empire — an amazing development.

The time period covered by the book of Esther was during the period of the restoration between the first return of the Jews to Israel, led by Zerubbabel, and the second, led by Ezra. A third return under Nehemiah came even later. The book of Esther is written in the form of a historical story. This makes it easy to see the work of God's providential hand to influence human events. Because of the plotting of the king's adviser, Haman, all the Jews still living in the provinces of Persia were to be killed. At that crucial point in time, Mordecai spoke to Esther, who had become, by the providence of

God, the queen of Persia. Mordecai, doubtless inspired by the Holy Spirit, perceived God's purpose in the elevation of Esther. We read in Esther 4:14:

> For if you remain completely silent at this time, relief and deliverance will arise for the Jews from another place, but you and your father's house will perish. *Yet who knows whether you have come to the kingdom for such a time as this?*

Queen Esther had become queen in order to fulfill a part of God's ongoing plan. At the moment of crisis, she decided to put her life on the line for her people. She sent this word back to Mordecai (Esther 4:16):

> Go, gather all the Jews who are present in Shushan, and fast for me; neither eat nor drink for three days, night or day. My maids and I will fast likewise. And so I will go to the king, which is against the law; and if I perish, I perish!

What happened was one of the most remarkable turns of events recorded in history. It began with a king who couldn't sleep. He called to have the "book of the records of the chronicles" brought to him. Thus the name "Mordecai" was brought back into the ongoing story of the king, just as the chief butler's memory brought the name of Joseph before Pharaoh. From the sleeplessness of King Ahasuerus, a series of events, directed by the hand of God, led to the placing of Queen Esther next to the King to plead for the lives of her people. Because of several God-directed events — the interpretation of dreams, several banquets, and the queen's intervention — Haman (the creator of the plot to kill the Jews in Persia) was hanged on the very gallows he had built to hang Mordecai.

Even though the Book of Esther is written entirely from the perspective of man's activity, one can clearly see God's hand working within the political government of Persia in order to fulfill His eternal plan. *God was involved. He was involved in putting Esther into the governmental structure of Persia in order to fulfill His will.*

Another explicit example of God's political involvement and the involvement of His people is evidenced by the life of Daniel. The prophet Daniel served politically in four governments under four different kings of two different empires. He served the Babylonian Empire under Nebuchadnezzar and Belshazzar and the Persian Empire under Darius and Cyrus. Daniel was taken captive when Nebuchadnezzar sacked Jerusalem. He rose to political prominence when the king sought young men with quick understanding from among the Hebrew captives, planning to teach them the culture and language of the Chaldeans. After three years of training (Daniel 1:20), Nebuchadnezzar tested and found Belteshazzar (Daniel), Shadrach, Meshach and Abednego *ten times greater* in wisdom and understanding than all the existing magicians and astrologers in his kingdom. In addition, God had given Daniel the ability to understand visions and dreams. That gift promptly played an important role, for King Nebuchadnezzar had a dream which troubled him deeply. In order to outsmart his sorcerers (who, he suspected, might give him a false interpretation), he refused to tell them the details of the dream, but required them, nevertheless, to interpret it for him under pain of death if they failed. Daniel and his companions were among them. Of course, the sorcerers could not interpret without the dream, so Nebuchadnezzar began to have all the wise men put to death (Daniel 2:13).

Daniel secured some time from the king so that he and his companions could seek God. God revealed the dream to Daniel in a night vision; Daniel then revealed the dream and interpretation to the King; it concerned a great image with toes of clay and iron mixed. The interpretation was a prophecy about several successive kingdoms which would rule, ending with God's everlasting kingdom. The King was greatly astonished and thus "...promoted Daniel and gave him many gifts; and he made him ruler over the whole province of Babylon, and chief administrator over all the wise men of Babylon" (Daniel 2:48).

Here we again see God's man in a place of governmental authority with God as an active participant in the affairs of mankind

— *using government and politics; even pagan governments and unrighteous political systems.*

If God allows us to be tempted and if, by the exercise of our own will, we respond by carrying out the action prompted by the temptation, are we released from the guilt and responsibility of that action? Of course not! Remember that a sin occurs only when we yield to the temptation. When we willingly participate with the temptation in thought, word or deed, then sin has been conceived. If we yield to a temptation that God has personally and directly allowed to come into our lives, we will not be able to plead *not guilty* on the grounds that someone else made us do it. We alone are responsible for our wrongdoing. If we resist temptation, we have then proved ourselves, by God's grace, to be overcomers in that area. If not, God will take us full circle and allow us to face the same situation until we draw enough strength from Him to overcome. In other words, we take another lap.

Scripture is bold and clear in stating that God uses the free-will choices of individuals and nations for His purposes and glory, while at the same time, judging them for the wrong they do. Jeremiah 51:7 says that "Babylon was a golden cup *in the Lord's hand*, that made all the earth drunk. The nations drank her wine; therefore the nations are deranged...." Then the end of verse 9 says, "...for her *judgment* reaches to heaven and is lifted up to the skies...." And verse 24 reads, "...and *I will repay* Babylon and all the inhabitants of Chaldea for all the evil they have done in Zion in your sight, says the Lord."

Even though God used Babylon, the people were personally accountable for the evil they did by their own choice. Everyone else is too, for as James 1:12 says, "[b]lessed is the man who endures temptation; *for* when *he has been approved*, he will receive the crown of life...."

What happens if we fail the test? Let us say that a man is attempting to overcome sexual lust and the Lord allows a seductive female to enter his life, and instead of standing strong against the temptation, the man fails and commits sin. Can the man say, "I did not sin?" No, of course not. He sinned, even though God allowed the circumstance. And what about the female who was the agent of temptation? By exercising her free will, she participated in the sin.

Is she then free from sin because God allowed the circumstance? No, of course not!

Let us imagine a commanding officer in the military, who orders a soldier to go into and secure a little town at the junction of two highways. While he is there, he robs the bank and does other wrongful acts. Is he guiltless because the officer sent him there? The Scripture says in Matthew 18:7: "Woe to the world because of offenses! For offenses must come, *but woe to that man by whom the offense comes!*" The word "offense" could easily be translated "enticements" which is also supported by the Greek definition. That is why the Amplified Bible translates this verse like this: "Woe to the world for such temptations to sin and influences to do wrong! It is *necessary* that temptations come, but woe to the person on whose account or by whom the temptation comes!"

That is the reason God could use Babylon's free-will errors to accomplish a purpose He desired and then, at the same time, hold Babylon accountable for exercising her free will to sin. In the same way, He holds accountable the man who submitted to sexual temptation, as well as the woman who brought the temptation into his life, even if God allowed or arranged the circumstances.

This same truth is seen in the Garden of Eden. The circumstances (i.e., the garden and its contents) were arranged by God. There existed a tree of the knowledge of good and evil. The fruit was pleasant to look at. In the Garden were also a cunning serpent, a man and a woman. The end result of this set of circumstances was temptation, sin and, subsequently, the fall of the human race into and under the dominance of the principle of sin itself. The response of the man and woman to God reinforces the points I am making. In answer to God's question, "... have you eaten from the tree of which I commanded you that you should not eat?" — the man said, "*The woman* whom *You* gave to be with me, she gave me of the tree, and I ate." (Genesis 3:11-12)

Adam's defense was to attempt to remove guilt from himself by blaming the person through whom his personal temptation came, "the woman" (Eve), as well as by placing the blame on the arranger of the circumstances, (the Lord God to whom he was talking). Remember, Adam said to God, "*[t]he woman whom You gave to be *with me,* she gave me of the tree and I ate." In essence Adam said, "Hey, you're the One who gave this woman to me, remember?" God's attention then rightly turns to the woman for she was the person who brought the temptation to Adam. Did God's change of focus alleviate Adam's sin? No, of course not, but to his credit Adam rightfully confessed when he said, " ... she gave me of the tree and *I ate.*" Eve also, like Adam, attempted to shift the blame. But, like Adam, she also confessed.

It is interesting that the Lord God did not ask the serpent a question, as He had asked the woman and the man. In addressing the serpent, God then started dispensing judgment, first to the serpent (Genesis 3:14-15), next to the woman (Genesis 3:16), and then to the man (Genesis 3:17).

The facts are simple: The serpent tempted the woman; she not only sinned by yielding to that temptation, but also tempted the man; the man sinned, but did not tempt anyone else, yet tried to blame God. All sinned, but each received different but equal justice from God. The judgment was based on the personal action of each individual. The tempter was judged on the fact that he tempted (i.e., "but woe to the man by whom the offense comes").

The people receiving the temptation were not judged on the fact that they were tempted, but on the fact that they did the wrong encouraged by the temptation.

Pointing out the tempter as the one who tempts us may be the truth, but blaming him for our action does not alter in the slightest our responsibility for the deed we did. Nor does blaming God, as Adam did (*"... the woman YOU gave me"*), because our circumstances did not commit the evil deed — we did. Only we determine our actions. *There may be strong influences, but an influence, by its very nature, is only an influence — not a decision. We make the decision to sin.*

Likewise, Babylon was a golden cup in the Lord's hands. Tempted by her splendor, the other nations failed the test and, by their own decision, became drunk on Babylon's excesses. Even though God allowed Babylon to advance and prosper, the decisions she made, she made on her own. They were her deeds. Even though God allowed Babylon to increase in dominion and success, whereby the nations became seduced, the decision to participate in Babylon's sins was still theirs alone. God used Babylon to test and judge others, but to do wrong was always Babylon's own decision, as it is with any nation or any individual.

God will use anything that exists to advance His eternal plan or to save the soul of one or many. He will use satan. He will use someone's sin. He will use a nation He has allowed to become successful. He will also judge the personal free-will actions of everyone, regardless of whether He uses those actions in the advancement of His own purposes.

He used the sin of Joseph's brothers to place Joseph in Egypt. Because God used their sin, should He not still hold them responsible for their free-will actions? It would be impossible for Him to not hold them responsible — for then He would cease to be God. Such an action would violate His holiness and, therefore, dispel the eternal truth that God is just.

We may then say He should not be involved in the affairs of men. Banish the thought, for we don't know what we are saying! If God were not actively involved, using everything that in His perfect wisdom and moral perfection he desires to use, we would not have been saved from our sins.

It is only God's ongoing activity that makes it possible for people to find Christ. John 6:44 says, "No one can come to me unless the Father who sent me draws him..."

Neither would there be a plan of redemption, because without God's active participation in all things and at every level, the devil would have wrapped up the whole situation in open rebellion and defiance toward God long ago. The truth of the matter is that we had all better fall on our knees and thank God that He *is* involved, and let Him know that we trust Him with the management of our existence, especially at this time in a world infected with sin, where the devil is roaming about.

It is essential that we believe that He is the One True God, the Lord God Almighty, and that we trust Him to use anything and anyone He wants, and to do anything He must, to redeem the greatest possible number of souls. It is essential that we believe that it is God's sovereign right (He is going to do so with or without our approval) to use the devil, individual reprobate humans, and even entire villages, tribes, cities and nations for His sovereign purposes.

In truth, everyone should be wholeheartedly thankful that God continues to be involved in the affairs of men. In fact, one's personal comfort with that idea reflects one's knowledge of Him. It is a measure of one's understanding of His righteousness, His moral purity and His divinity. It reveals the level and the quality of one's faith and trust in Him as God.

We can be sure that, with or without man's faith in Him, He will use the *"vessels of wrath prepared for destruction"* (all who failed their tests). When tested, they proved their personal loyalty and commitment to the sin that entered the Garden of Eden so many years ago. "And even as they did not like to retain God in their knowledge, *God gave them over the a reprobate mind*, to do those things which are not convenient" (Romans 1:28 KJV). The word "reprobate" in the Greek is "adokimos,*"* and its literal meaning is "not standing the test,"[1] thus unqualified or rejected. Reprobate persons are the "vessels of wrath fitted for destruction."

Remember, one of God's unique attributes is that He knows the future. Even though He has obligated Himself to interact with mankind in our present limited state, it does not diminish the full capacities of His own eternal and unlimited existence. No matter how difficult it is for us to understand, the Scripture is clear — God knows all things, even the future. In Acts 2:23, while speaking of Jesus, Peter says, "Him, being delivered by the determined purpose *and foreknowledge of God*, you have taken by lawless hands, have crucified, and put to death."

God has foreknowledge. Without going into all the implications of that fact, we must accept that God knows what is going to happen. So when the scripture says, "God turned them over," that is a statement reflecting His activity within the lower concurrent level of our existence, where He has obligated Himself to work within the realm of man, taking mankind's inherent limitations into consideration. As a result of His activity, reprobate persons have failed the test. Instead of choosing God, they have given themselves completely to sin, and God has released them to their choice. It is only the beginning of the reality of hell, although hell is a place where absolutely no godly influence remains — not a single trace.

Simultaneously, on the second or higher level, because of His foreknowledge, God already knows who is who. That is why the Holy Spirit can call these individuals reprobate — rejected, unredeemable. However, they could not be in this state except as a result of their free-will action, for Scripture clearly reveals in Romans 1:21 the first step in that process. "...*although they knew God, they did not glorify Him as God, nor were thankful, but became futile in their thoughts and their foolish hearts were darkened.*" Verse 23 describes the continuing process. "...*and change the glory of the incorruptible God into an image made like corruptible man...*" The result is given in verse 24, *("Therefore God also gave them up ...")* and continues in verse 26. *"For this reason God gave them up to vile passions."* Then the final portion of the process, which begins and ends with the free-will actions of man, is found in verse 28. "And *even as they did not like to retain* God in their knowledge, *God gave them over* to a debased (KJV: reprobate) mind."

Even though God deals with man in reality at man's level, He knows already who will accept His rightful authority and, conversely, who will give himself solely to himself. That is why the Lord said to the Apostle Paul, who was preaching at Corinth, in Acts 18:9-10, "... Do not be afraid, but speak, and do not keep silent; for I am with you, and no one will attack you to hurt you; *for I have many people in this city.*"

Even before the preaching that still had to be done; even before the conviction and then the forgiveness of sins; even before the accepting of Christ as Lord and Savior; God knew which people would choose rightly. That is the foreknowledge of God. Even before He allows the process of testing, God knows those who will ultimately fail the tests, failing to be proven, who will, by their own actions, reach the point at which God knows they have irrevocably given themselves over to sin. He then turns them over to the unredeemable mind which they have chosen for themselves, the condition in which He calls them "vessels of wrath prepared for destruction." Even in that condition, however, God may use them by putting circumstances into their lives, allowing them to exercise their free will in a manner that God can use for His own purposes, to bring either judgment or benefit to others.

Without God's intervention in the affairs of man, we (those of us who have accepted God's gift in Christ Jesus) would not be saved since without God's involvement, Christ would not have come to fulfill His key role in the unfolding eternal plan of God.

In like manner, God used the sinful decisions of the people of Babylon, but He also judged those same sinful decisions because they were made as a result of the working of the free will. That is the reason Babylon could be a "golden cup *in the Lord's hand*" and at the same time God can say in Jeremiah 50:31, "Behold, I am against you, O most haughty one! says the Lord of Hosts; For your day has come, The time that I will punish you." Even though God used Babylon to bring judgment to Israel, Jeremiah 51:53 says, "Though Babylon were to mount up to heaven, and though she were to fortify the height of her strength, Yet *from me* plunderers would come to her, says the Lord."

God, because He is God, has a right to call for an accounting from any portion of His creation at any time He pleases. This fact is not a subject for debate. We may argue it, but God's sovereignty is not affected by our questioning of it. For this is the most essential question for each free-will entity to answer: is He God? Is He just a super entity, merely a collective consciousness, or is He the Lord God Almighty, creator of Heaven and earth, the One True God? " ... for he who comes to God must believe that *He is....*" *(Hebrews 11:6)*

As for me, I believe that He is: that He is the sovereign God and He is perfect in holiness. These are the defining characteristics of God. He did not mature into this position, He simply always is. He will do with His creation as He sees fit. As a free-will entity, I acknowledge that *He has "power over the clay."* And, at the same time, that He *"cannot be tempted by evil, nor does He Himself tempt anyone."* However, He does put everyone to the test, and He does use the results of testing both to advance His Kingdom and to judge each man's moral capacity: his ability as a free-willed, living soul to make the choices that will determine his eternal condition.

Daniel understood this. As we saw in chapter one, he did not think it was unusual that God gave a prophetic dream to the very king who destroyed Jerusalem and looted God's temple. I am convinced Daniel felt both sorrow and anger about what had happened to his homeland as well as the condition of his own life. However, Daniel exhibited more spiritual maturity than do the vast majority of Christians today. He understood completely (his understanding ruled and ordered his attitude and behavior) that what happened to Israel, the temple and himself was due to the collective actions of the Hebrews themselves. What happened to the inhabitants of Jerusalem resulted from what they did. They had failed the test God gave them; He would not be God if He did not judge. The circumstances and the timing did not matter. What mattered now to Daniel was his own ongoing relationship with God.

Like Daniel, and Joseph before him, we must commit ourselves to God and serve Him with all our heart, might and soul, no matter what our circumstances.

From Daniel's actions and attitude, we can confidently assume He understood the concept of the justice of God and of eternal judgment. In Daniel 4, the idea that God ruled actively over the kingdom of Babylon, regardless of its iniquities was no doctrinal surprise to Daniel.

Whether he wants to acknowledge the truth or not, even the worst sinner walking this earth is still under the authority of God (a fact which will one day become painfully clear to him).

Daniel knew also that the people of Babylon, just like any other nation or any single individual, will one day have to give account for their sins, whether in this life or in eternity. It did not surprise Daniel theologically when God moved politically to raise him and the others into governmental positions in that pagan empire. Nor should it surprise us that both God and His people were politically involved. Joseph, Esther, Moses, Shadrach, Meshach, Abednego and Daniel were all involved with God, as were many others, in the political affairs of different nations.

It is clear that God is politically involved. So are His people.

Chapter 3

God Owns Civil Government

"Let every soul be subject to the governing authorities. *For there is no authority except from God, and the authorities that exist are appointed by God.*" (Romans 13:1)

This Scripture states one of those fundamental and cardinal principles of existence: God Himself is the source of all authority. Just as He is the source of all life, all created matter and all spiritual substance and beings, He is also the source of all authority.

Authority residing with one and subsequently given to another to be exercised is called *delegated authority.* Earlier we saw that this is what Pharaoh did with Joseph. He delegated his own authority as king of Egypt. The same type of delegation occurred in the case of King Nebuchadnezzar and Daniel.

The Apostle Paul is saying to us in Romans 13:1 that God Himself delegated authority to be used for governing. For the Scripture says clearly that "governing" or *civil* authority is from God. No authority exists unless it is established by God. The NIV translates the phrase as saying, "...there is no authority except that which God has established." Phillip's Modern English translation says, "...for all legitimate authority is derived from God's authority..." James Moffatt translates, "...no authority exists apart from God..."

Government is an institution or sphere of authority, accountability and responsibility which was created, established and instituted by God Himself. In order to understand the economy and providence of God, a person needs to thoroughly understand this passage of Scripture.

There are certain truths or foundational principles upon which everything created by God operates. Contained in these truths and principles is a group of three spheres of delegated authority established by God. Each of these spheres is intended to guide a specific area of man's function upon this earth. A good understanding of these spheres will ensure the well-being of any society or government.

The first sphere of delegated authority is recorded in Genesis 2:23 & 24:

> And Adam said: "This is now bone of my bones and flesh of my flesh; she shall be called Woman, because she was taken out of Man." Therefore a man shall leave his father and mother and be joined to his wife, and they shall become one flesh.

It also appears in Ephesians 6:1-4:

> Children, obey your parents in the Lord, for this is right. Honor your father and mother, which is the first commandment with promise: that it may be well with you and you may live long on the earth. And you, fathers, do not provoke your children to wrath, but bring them up in the training and admonition of the Lord.

The family is the first and most fundamental and essential institution or sphere of delegated authority, created and established by God. Its bases are the romantic and sexual affection between a man and a woman, and also their nurturing relationship to any children produced by their union. Under God, the family structure, operating in good order, is the vital element necessary for cultural and social health. The autonomy and proper functioning of the family is the number one social consideration. When the families of a community are not functioning properly in every respect, at a level which allows all their members to enjoy such basic benefits as love, acceptance, security, correction and character building, we lose the only institution designed to supply stability and the ingredients necessary to produce social health in the larger community.

The parents are responsible before God to raise, correct, love and educate their children. And God has delegated authority to the parents to accomplish this.

The second sphere of delegated authority established by God was that of religious authority. Under the Old Covenant, that authority centered around the temple, the Levitical priesthood (the Law) and the synagogue. But when the New Covenant was established at the death and resurrection of Jesus, that authority was vested by God in the Church. The Church's authority operates in matters of a spiritual nature — in areas of morality, seeking and interpreting God's will, and in fulfilling the mandate and purpose of God through the teaching of salvation, discipleship, care and compassion.

God has entrusted the Church to be "the pillar and ground of the truth" (I Timothy 3:15). The word "ground" is defined as "foundation" or "mainstay." The Church is God's vehicle of spiritual truth in and for this world. It is to be the advocate and defender of morality, righteousness and truth, and it has the authority from God to be these things.

The third sphere of authority delegated by God deals with another arena of human life — civil government. Romans 13:1 starts out by saying: "Let every soul be subject to the governing authority ..." This includes every living human being. All mankind is to be subject to civil authority. The word "subject" in the Greek is "hupotasso," a military term meaning to rank, arrange, or array under. Synonyms would be "obedient" or "submitted or "subdued." The power of this earthly institution, as intended by God, is indeed formidable!

Since there may be some who take exception here, let me restate the premise: civil authority, like religious authority and family authority, is delegated by God Himself for a purpose. Such authority is not absolute authority, since it is delegated to human individuals who are capable of misusing it. Therefore, each user is accountable to God for his administration of such delegated authority as he holds, and he is held to a higher standard than the person who holds none, i.e., "...to whom much is given, much is required" (Luke 12:48). (Also, see James 3:1)

At the same time, when the one entrusted with that authority exercises it in the manner God intended, the authority has the full weight and power of God behind it. To oppose it is to oppose God. The Apostle states this clearly in Romans 13:2: "Therefore whoever resists the authority resists the ordinance of God, and those who resist will bring judgment on themselves." (The word "ordinance" in the Greek is "diatage." Although the word "ordinance," when we consider the divine origin of the authority, is a good translation of the word "diatage," it could have been translated "decree of God," or "that which God ordained or appointed.") I prefer the NIV translation of this particular verse. It reads: "Consequently, he who rebels against the authority is rebelling against what God has instituted ...." The New English Bible captures this correct expression also: "... There is no authority but by act of God, and the existing authorities are instituted by Him; consequently anyone who rebels against authority is resisting *a divine institution* ...." The Amplified reads: "Therefore he who resists and sets himself up against the authorities resists what God has appointed and arranged — *in divine order.*"

This is obviously a divine truth: God formed civil government by the delegation of a portion of His own authority. Therefore, the authority contained in civil government is God's authority. Because it is God's authority, it is both instituted by God and accountable to Him to accomplish His intended purpose. Romans 13:3 says: "For rulers are not a terror to good works, but to evil ...."

God placed within the institution of civil government this cardinal principle which is its foundational and operational directive: government is to be a terror to evil; it is not to be a terror to good. Since the authority to accomplish this divine task is from God, He is also the standard for determining what is good and what is evil. God alone defines good and evil. Notice how the Apostle, through the Holy Spirit, states the operational standard for civil government in a very elementary way, the simplest of moral expressions; good and evil, right and wrong.

This does not mean, as some would have us believe, that there should be a full and complete reinstituting of the Mosaic Law. The scriptures make it abundantly clear that God has no desire to reestablish the Mosaic Law. He sent His own Son, Jesus, to die on a cross to get us out from under that same law, that we might obtain salvation through faith in His Son, not by the works of the Law. In Romans 13:3, God clearly states the operational standard for civil government under the New Covenant: to praise good and punish evil. Much of the *morality* expressed in the Mosaic Law, however, is transferable to civil law.

To further understand the first sentence of Romans 13:3, let us look at the word "terror," which in the Greek is "phobos," meaning "fear." More precisely in its usage here, it means that which causes fear, a degree of fear great enough to cause one to take flight. Thus, the word used is "terror." Civil authority is ordained by God to be a terror to evil.

The last two sentences of verse 3 describe in more detail civil government's relationship to good: "... Do you want to be unafraid of the authority? Do what is good, and you will have praise from the same." Civil government is to give open commendation or approbation to those engaged in doing good. As ordained by God, civil government's most basic operational mandate is to be a terror to evil works and a source of praise for what is good.

As noted above, the family, the Church and civil government are the three major foundational spheres of delegated authority. They are divinely-created institutions, formed to handle the activities of man. The family is to handle the relational needs of all individuals. The Church is to handle the spiritual needs. Civil government is to handle community order. Each sphere has a mandate and the delegated authority to fulfill its specific task. Because each has its own mandate, task and purpose, each is limited in what it can and should do. Each has its own prescribed area of responsibility and its own specific authority. When one sphere attempts to perform the tasks entrusted to one of the other two, this infringement usually causes damage that ends up hurting people.

For example, in God's economy which institution has responsibility to take care of those in need? I Timothy 5:8 reads: "But if anyone does not provide for his own, and especially for *those of his household*, he has denied the faith and is worse than an unbeliever." In God's order, the first level of responsibility and provision is the family caring for its own. If some fall through the netting, however, I Timothy 5:16 says: "If any believing man or woman has widows, let them relieve them, and do not let the church be burdened, *that it may relieve those who are really widows.*" The second line of provision according to this scripture is the Church. This is clear also in Galatians 2:10 where, speaking of the Jerusalem Apostles' recognition of Paul's ministry to the Gentiles, Paul says: "They desired only that we should remember the poor, *the very thing which I also was eager to do.*"

There are numerous other scriptural references that place the responsibility to provide for those in need on the family, the Church and the individual (e.g., the good Samaritan). This is God's economy. His word declares His desires and establishes His design.

Yet who in our culture has taken over the responsibility to care for the needy? The civil government has. Is this shift in responsibility working? No! It is an absolute disaster. Trillions of dollars are being poured down a hole, lost forever, only to produce a society with more poverty and economic dependency than there was at the time that government began to violate God's requirements. When one sphere of delegated authority, one of God's divine institutions, attempts to use the authority delegated to one of the other divine institutions, people are usually hurt rather than helped. This has been clearly evident throughout history when the Church has usurped the authority of civil government (e.g., persecution of other religious groups, inquisitions, people burned at the stake).

An example from recent years involves the shepherding, discipleship movement of the 1970's. In my opinion (and I have first-hand knowledge), sincere men and women brought too much of the authority delegated specifically for the Church into the sphere of the family. Though there are legitimate, Biblical and God-ordained discipleship, shepherding and covenant relationships, they were never meant to usurp the delegated authority of the family by taking the place of the father's or mother's role in decision-making. Rather, the mandate and function of the Church is the teaching of Godly principles to the Body of Christ, giving family members the tools to function effectively in a Christian family. With this out of balance, people suffer.

God delegated specific portions of His authority to broad fundamental arenas to provide optimum benefit and social order for mankind. To enjoy the benefit, each sphere must concern itself with the fulfillment of its own mandate and the proper use of its own specific delegated authority.

We saw in Romans 13:3 that the primary function of civil government is to be a terror to evil and a rewarder of good. Civil government is an institution established by God, who has delegated authority to man to carry out governmental functions. This is all part of God's design and based on His will. It works because civil government is really God's own authority in action within a community. Romans 13:4 reveals the truth of that statement. Speaking about the civil leader, the Scripture says, *"For he is God's minister to you for good ...."*

Civil authority is an institution created and maintained by God. People actively involved in using that authority are called "God's ministers." The Holy Spirit says that those entrusted with God's delegated authority (for the purpose of carrying on civil government) are administering something that is divine in origin. What are they administering on God's behalf? It is His delegated authority to deal with the behavior of people as they live and relate to one another in a community setting.

For example, if your neighbor throws garbage over your fence, you do not call your mom to deal with the problem, do you? Nor do you call your pastor, for which he is surely grateful. God created civil government for this type of problem. It is government's role in God's grand design to deal with the behavior and conduct of human beings in a social, community setting. According to Romans 13:4, on behalf of God, this is what they minister:

> For he is God's minister to you *for good*. But if you do evil, be afraid; for he does not bear the sword in vain; for *he is God's minister, an avenger to execute wrath on him who practices evil.*

It is imperative to remember that there are two primary but equal and coexistent aspects to God's love. These qualities are probably best described by the two words "mercy" and "judgment." Often an individual tends to major in one and minor in, if even acknowledging, the other. Yet in God, such an imbalance is not a desired condition, and is only arrived at when fallen human nature has sway. When God expresses His love, the decision as to which quality of His love is expressed — mercy or judgment — depends upon what the recipient is doing, not upon weakness within God (if such a thing were possible). Whenever there is a place, time or situation in which a choice can be made opposite to the moral purity of God, there will exist equally, the ability and willingness for God to express divine judgment.

While the opportunity to make eternal decisions is available to man, the divine prerogative of moral judgment is also available to be used by God at any time to punish wrongful conduct against anyone who occupies *His* creation. God's expression toward individuals who have fallen under His judgment, being found guilty by doing deeds contrary to His divine nature, is wrath. Without intervention, such as repentance and forgiveness, the consequence of wrongdoing will be God's wrath. God's wrath is an absolute. It is an automatic extension of holiness. Where there is no divine wrath, there is no moral perfection; therefore, because He is God, He must manifest wrath against those who commit ungodliness and refuse to repent.

This expression of God's wrath is a moral absolute vital to the eternal good order of the universe, God has delegated its function into the form of civil government for the prevention of disorder among human beings as they interact with one another. God placed within the framework of civil government the delegated divine authority to be an "avenger."

This is a significant truth because God is circumspect about the action of vengeance. Yet, here we see that one of the main functions of civil government is to exercise vengeance. Vengeance, in its proper role, serves God's justice. No one should be disturbed that vengeance is associated with God (see Romans 12:19). His vengeance is simply an expression of divine justice, the retribution which evil demands. In fact, if punishment wasn't rendered in a manner proportionate to the evil manifested, divine justice would be nullified, and God would no longer be God. Vengeance *compensates* for evil, thus maintaining righteousness. This is part of the divine nature because the divine nature is holy and pure and righteous altogether. The divine nature is the essence of God. The divine nature does not *rule* Him; He *is* the divine nature. God is love, but contained in that love is both mercy and justice because the love of God is a perfect love. This reality is inescapable. It is immutable. Romans 2:2-3 reads:

> But we know that the judgment of God is according to truth against those who practice such things. (author's note: "such things" are Romans 1:21-32) And do you think this, O Man, you who judge those practicing such things, and doing the same, that you will escape the judgment of God?

And verse 6 adds: "Who will render to each according to his deeds." Judgment, retribution and vengeance are as certain as is God Himself. His love, perfection and holiness demand such. Because these qualities are Who God is, He will judge and reward or punish each of us according to our deeds. But He has also supplied a way out of this unavoidable dilemma of our sinfulness facing His holiness. Jesus Christ personally paid the price for all "such things" (i.e., all of our sins) by His death on the cross. At the end of the day, as the last sentence of James 2:13 says, *"Mercy triumphs over judgment."*

To receive His mercy, however, we must accept the sacrifice of Christ, enthroning the Lord Jesus in our hearts; this is God's merciful answer to the problem of sin. Sin, after all, consists of our acts of rebellion and defiance, which are contrary to the divine nature, the holiness of Almighty God. God must respond to sin in one way or the other: with mercy or with vengeance.

God has delegated to civil authority a measure of His own *attributes* which will expose every idle word, reveal every action done in secret, and make known every thought, motive and intent of every heart. Those same attributes are inherent in God's delegated authority and give the driving motivation to those who have taken responsibility in the civil arena to seek out and punish evildoers. In the Greek, the word "avenger" is "ekdikos," meaning an exactor of full justice. Literally, it means, "... avenging, subst. the avenger, the one who punishes ..."[1]

God requires civil government to perform the task of vengeance — its prime directive. This is true to such a degree that the Holy Spirit calls those who dispense this particular type of delegated authority "God's ministers." Obviously they are not ministers of the Gospel in the same way that a pastor is, but in the performance of their duties as civil officials they "minister" civil authority, delegated by God, with the requirements and mandates contained therein.

Civil government is an arena distinct in its purpose, and functionally very different from the Church and the family. Just as the Church is to influence, support, help and teach the family without replacing the family or exercising the authority placed within the family, the Church is to influence, support and teach civil government and to hold it accountable. Again, the Church is not to replace the civil government or exercise the authority placed therein. By the same token, each sphere of authority is not to replace or improperly intrude into the authority of the others.

The truth is clear — God is very much involved in civil government, and those who perform its duties are to be considered "His ministers."

These absolutes should help us to look a little differently at those who hold the offices of president, senator, governor, mayor, city councilman, and school board member. It also introduces questions. How are they using God's authority? What are they establishing with God's authority? Are they using God's authority for the purposes for which it was delegated? Or are they using God's own authority to promote and sanction public policy which is actually contrary to God's divine nature?

Scripture is clear in stating what should be the operating premise of civil government. Government is to reward and encourage good, while it is to be a terror to evil. Civil authority is to bear the sword. It is to avenge wrongdoing, to execute wrath on those who practice evil. Romans 13:6-7 end this passage of Scripture by saying:

> For *because of this* you also pay taxes, for *they are God's ministers attending continually to this very thing.* Render therefore to all their due: taxes to whom taxes are due, customs to whom customs, fear to whom fear, honor to whom honor.

The Apostle and the Holy Spirit leave no room to view the institution of government and those carrying out the duties thereof in any way other than this: government is God's delegated authority for the maintenance of good over evil in the social interaction of a community. And those performing this function are "His ministers."
God is politically active!

If He Himself is politically involved, would He then turn to His people and tell them not to be involved or active in the very institution that He has created, and within which He maintains personal activity?

God did not tell Esther to stay out of politics. God did not tell Joseph, or Daniel, or Shadrach, Meshach and Abednego that government involvement is off-limits to believers. No, the opposite is true! God Himself anointed these people, set up circumstances, and was actively involved in leading them among the political affairs of their nations. Romans 13 tells us why: Government itself, in its reason for being, in its very essence, is from God. Why wouldn't He feel at ease working within its confines? Why wouldn't His people feel fully at ease working within their governments as well? Daniel did! So did the others. And so should we, unless we have been taught contrary to these principles which God has laid out in His Word.

We will discuss the problem of government promotion of evil, and our response to it, in a later chapter. Let us close this chapter by citing another passage of Scripture, this one written by a different apostle, at a different time and to a different group of believers. In I Peter 2:13-14 we read:

> Therefore submit yourselves to every ordinance of man for the Lord's sake, whether to the king as

supreme, or to governors, as to those who are *sent by Him for the punishment of evildoers and for the praise of those who do good.*

Civil leaders are *"...those sent by <u>HIM</u>..."* God is politically involved!

Chapter 4

The Prophet John The Baptist

John the Baptist had been called of God to fulfill a most important and specific ministry. He had been given the task of preparing the way of the Messiah. We see in the Scriptures that he fulfilled his divine assignment perfectly. He seems to have profoundly affected the whole culture in which he lived. Matthew 3:5 indicates this when it says: "Then Jerusalem, all Judea, and all the region around the Jordan went out to him and were baptized by him in the Jordan, confessing their sins." The indication is that his ministry greatly and positively impacted his nation as he went about preparing the way for Christ.

Yet John's public witness also brought him into confrontation with the religious leaders of his day, and even with the civil authority. The religious leaders had made their way down to the river's edge to see the wild-looking prophet about whom everyone was talking. Focusing directly on those leaders in Matthew 3:7-12, John forcefully and directly said:

> ... Brood of vipers! Who warned you to flee from the wrath to come? Therefore bear fruits worthy of repentance, and do not think to say to yourselves, "We have Abraham as our father." For I say to you that God is able to raise up children to Abraham from these stones. And even now the ax is laid to the root of the trees. Therefore every tree which does not bear good fruit is cut down and thrown into the fire. I indeed baptize you with water unto

repentance, but He who is coming after me is mightier than I, whose sandals I am not worthy to carry. He will baptize you with the Holy Spirit and fire. His winnowing fan is in His hand, and He will thoroughly clean out His threshing floor, and gather His wheat into the barn; but He will burn up the chaff with unquenchable fire.

Needless to say, this was a stinging attack which John the Baptist aimed directly at the religious leaders of his day. In modern times, John would be labeled mean-spirited by the world, and lacking Christian compassion by believers. But it was the mission God had given him, and not the opinion of men, that mattered to John.

John the Baptist was obviously aware of what Jesus would later describe as the "leaven of the Pharisees," hypocrisy. John rightfully challenged the sincerity of what was motivating their actions. It was part of both Jesus' and John's ministry to expose these men's motives because of their position of authority and influence over so many souls. What must be remembered is the nature of the conflict and the stakes at risk. These religious leaders (I use the word religious in its generic or human sense, because they were not even loyal to orthodox Judaism) were deceiving the people. Later in the scriptures Jesus said to the same type of leaders in Matthew 23:13: "But woe to you, scribes and Pharisees, hypocrites! For you shut up the kingdom of heaven against men; for you neither go in yourselves, nor do you allow those who are entering to go in." This reveals what John himself had also earlier perceived. Jesus continues in verses 29-33:

> Woe to you, scribes and Pharisees, hypocrites! Because you build the tombs of the Prophets and adorn the monuments of the righteous, and say, "If we had lived in the days of our fathers, we would not have been partakers with them in the blood of the Prophets." Therefore you are witnesses against yourselves that you are sons of those who murdered the Prophets. *Fill up, then, the measure of*

your father's guilt. Serpents, brood of vipers! How can you escape the condemnation of hell?

This statement of Jesus clearly reveals God's heart and his position on the subject of spiritual and moral confrontation. God has revealed His own nature by sending His own Son, who offered Himself as a sacrifice and payment for our sinfulness. At the same time and with equal resolve, He acts in a manner that forces the issue of whom we serve, what we do, and where we are going to spend eternity.

This forcing of the issue is clearly seen in Revelation 3:15-16 and Matthew 7:17-19. In both scriptures Jesus states His preference that people be either good or bad, hot or cold. In the Revelation, He says: "...I could wish you were cold or hot. So then, because you are lukewarm, and neither cold nor hot, *I will vomit you out of my mouth."*

Jesus was saying to the religious leaders in Matthew 23 that if you are going to be *cold*, fill yourselves ("fill up") completely with cold. The particular cold referred to was that which led their fathers to murder the prophets.

In the eternal perspective of God, there is no lukewarm or middle area, only the vastly different alternatives: Heaven and hell. In the former there is only obedience; in the latter, only rebellion. In Heaven there is God — in hell, satan. The drawing of the line which divides these two distinct and eternal conditions occurred when Jesus came to earth and set into motion God's heavenly and mysterious plan. This *either/or* principle is also seen when Jesus said in Matthew 12:30: "He who is not with Me is against Me, and he who does not gather with Me scatters abroad." It is clearly one or the other — there is no gray area. From the moment Jesus put into motion God's plan at the beginning of His own ministry, the requirement was the same — either hot or cold. We are either for Him or against Him. Either we gather or we scatter. Lukewarmness is not an acceptable attitude in Christ. This particular position is an absolute, and not negotiable. It is established and promoted by God Himself.

Sin will be dealt with once and for all. It will be completely purged out of believers because we want it to be, and because He demands that it be. It is also true that those who refuse Christ, desiring instead to have and enjoy their sin, will get their wish. But this we must know — ultimately in God's creation, righteousness will reign. Likewise, in hell, separated from God and all that He is, sin will reign. But at that time, unlike in this present age, sin will reign devoid of any Godly influence or restraint. Because man's choice between the two realms is for eternity, the stakes are as high as they can be. That is why Christ was so hard on those who were working against God's Messiah and thus against His will and plan.

Having knowledge of God's plan is what prompted John the Baptist to challenge the religious leaders of his day. He represented God's truth on this earth, as did Jesus. Compelled by that truth, each of them put forward God's standards and policies with submission, passion and sincerity. So must anyone who is called by God as His representative, or anyone who makes that claim.

It is evident that God hates any kind of mixture resulting in lukewarmness. To Him, the middle-of-the-road, wishy-washy, lukewarm attitude is so unsavory that His response is to spew, spit or vomit it out (depending on how we translate the Greek word, *Emeo*). The word expresses God's extreme displeasure at that mixture of hot and cold. Why? Once again, it is because the stakes are extremely high. The condition of a person's soul for all of eternity is what is in harm's way; therefore, God will not tolerate halfway measures in our representation of His truth and light.

The religious leaders of John's day were guiding their followers on a path leading away from God. Therefore, it was incumbent upon God's representative on earth to point this out to them in the strongest terms. This would enable all concerned to receive proper warning, giving them the greatest opportunity to correct their actions, if they so desired. Like Jesus, John had correctly discerned that the motivation of these leaders' teaching was to guide people, not into the Kingdom of God, but rather the contrary. Therefore, in accordance with God's nature, the prophet gave them the warning that was needed — a direct confrontation with the truth.

It is important to remember that God was able to speak this strong word to the religious leaders because He had a prophet on the earth. Having direct representation on the earth enables God's will to be expressed as He wants it expressed. From God's perspective, the worst situation is that in which He has no direct representation (no individuals submitted wholly to God's will) expressing His eternal values. With no submitted representation of God's standard, millions of eternal decisions will be made, while God's actual position is not being *publicly* presented. Those decisions will occur without the benefit of God's direct influence supplied in a way that affects, to the greatest degree, their immediate circumstances. That is the importance of this kind of public stand. This principle of a public expression is emphasized over and over again in the scriptures, such as Matthew 10:32-33: "Therefore whoever confesses Me *before men,* him I will also confess before My Father who is in heaven. But whoever denies Me *before men,* him I will also deny before My Father who is in heaven."

Although this scripture refers specifically to faith being confessed or denied, the underlying principle of requiring a *public* expression is undeniable. This is seen some time later when Peter denied the Lord *publicly* ("before men"). The subject of the denial was that of knowing or being associated with Jesus — Mark 14:66-72. This public expression by Peter was negative in content, but the concept holds true for the positive as well. Matthew 5:16 says: "Let your light so shine *before men*, that they may see your good works and glorify your Father in heaven." Here the subject of the public expression is the *light* described in the Beatitudes, a reflection of the very nature of God Himself. "Pure in heart...meekness... peacemakers." Stated another way, this is the fruit of the Spirit, the very image of Jesus Christ. Yet, most tend to forget that part of the "good works" referred to in verse 16 above includes Beatitude number eight in Matthew 5:10, which says: "*Blessed are those who are persecuted for righteousness' sake, for theirs is the kingdom of heaven.*" Hardly anyone has a problem with the first seven Beatitudes. It would be rare indeed to be persecuted for being a "peacemaker," *but there is a stand for righteousness that will produce persecution.* There are two contextual keys in Matthew 5:11-12 which shed the needed light in comprehending this stand:

> Blessed are you when they revile and persecute you,

and say all kinds of evil against you falsely for My sake. Rejoice and be exceedingly glad, for great is your reward in Heaven, for so they persecuted the prophets who were before you.

The prophets were persecuted because they publicly challenged the wicked moral or spiritual conditions of their culture or of the governing authority of their day. Persecution was the consequence of their public stand "for righteousness' sake." Jesus used the example of these early prophets to indicate to His followers that they could expect the same phenomenon to befall His New Testament believers.

In verse eleven, Jesus said that all of these things would happen to us "for *My* sake." Jesus knew that when His people began to press His divine claims upon the society at large, they would run headlong into another kingdom, a kingdom established in defiance of and in open rebellion toward God, a kingdom established on principles of ungodliness. This encounter would be the breeding ground for the persecution, revilings and false accusations to which Jesus referred.

This type of public stand "for righteousness' sake," defended and advocated by Jesus in Matthew 5, is confrontation in its purest form. John the Baptist took such a stand in confronting the self-deceived religious leaders with God's truth and His standards. Any public declaration of a righteous standard will cause a negative reaction, either immediately or eventually, and result in some form of persecution from those who are unwilling to comply with God's standards.

As Jesus declared, such a public stand "for righteousness' sake," one which provokes persecution, is an action that is considered "blessed" in the kingdom of God. In fact, from God's perspective, if our public stand for righteousness causes us to receive persecution, He says in Matthew 5:12: "Rejoice and be exceedingly glad, for great is your reward in heaven...."

Why is persecution esteemed so highly in the outworking of God's plan for the earth during this present age? Surely it is unpleasant to endure persecution. But even during persecution, we are to be glad and rejoice in our circumstances. There can be only one reason for this — divine truth, or light, or righteousness, is being publicly expressed in a manner which God has judged necessary for the salvation of souls. This persecution indicates that someone is publicly representing God to the degree that He, as God, deserves to be represented. Such a public witness is bound to have the greatest positive impact on the eternal decisions being made by millions of people.

As Jesus experienced, eternity demanded the greatest personal sacrifice. Likewise, the eternal decisions being made by human beings demand the greatest degree of public witness, especially witness *"for righteousness' sake."* The public stand for what is right is absolutely vital and essential to the process of keeping the greatest number of souls from being eternally lost.

As we saw in the previous chapters, the most important truth that exists is God's claim upon and over the creation — God's sovereignty over all things. The outworking of that truth in His creation is the public witness which stands for good over evil and right over wrong. Without this witness, the message of God's people is impotent. Who will take the Christian message seriously if confessing Christians will not publicly stand up for what they believe to be the overriding principle in time and in eternity? Standing up for what He says is right demonstrates to the world the absolute sovereignty of God and our relationship of trust and obedience to Him. When we do this without regard for personal consequences, we lead others to a right relationship with Him as well. And if we are not leading souls into a right relationship with the holy and sovereign God of all existence, then where are we leading them?

Let me define that overriding principle. When all else is removed, the morally perfect and divine nature of the One True God remains, and the qualities of the divine nature emanate eternally from Him to permeate the whole of existence. This is divine righteousness. This righteousness establishes the morality of good over evil (right over wrong) as the ethical absolute of our universe — in fact, of all existence. This is known by many as natural law.

Being persecuted *"for righteousness' sake"* comes because we, His people, publicly attest that He is God, and affirm the absolute authority of His divine nature — His righteousness over our actions and His will over our lives as well as over every living soul that breathes His air. His people are His representatives on the earth.

Having established Beatitude number eight in Matthew 5 and further defining its scope and meaning in verses 11 and 12, let us read in context this famous scripture in Matthew 5:13. Jesus said:

> You are the salt of the earth; but if the salt loses its flavor, how shall it be seasoned? It is then good for nothing but to be thrown out and trampled underfoot by men.

This scripture also establishes the public nature of a stand for righteousness. It does not say we are the salt of the Church for the Church itself is the salt. Nor are we the salt of heaven for heaven does not need any salt. But we are the salt of the earth. The earth is what needs the salt. In God's opinion, the earth needs our witness regarding His righteousness. The following verses, 14 through 16 continue this train of thought:

> You are the light of the world. A city that is set on a hill cannot be hidden. Nor do they light a lamp and put it under a basket, but on a lampstand, and it gives light to all who are in the house. Let your light so shine before men, that they may see your good works and glorify your Father in heaven.

Jesus is clearly stating His requirement that we publicly represent God. This requirement includes not only our role as peacemakers in our witness of Him, but also the public stand for righteousness expressed in Beatitude number eight. The complete witness is described by Jesus as a city set on a hill, visible to everyone, and including both the non-confrontational and the confrontational expressions of Christianity.

The life of Mother Teresa contains examples of both types of expression, each of which was met by different reactions. It did not bother anyone that Mother Teresa did good deeds in India, but people became upset when she told our president that abortion was wrong. From her persistence and courage we can infer that she understood what Jesus was saying in Matthew 8:13-16. God requires a complete representation of Himself to this earth. He expects the full spectrum of His light to shine out to the whole world. That is why verse 15 says: *"Nor do they light a lamp and put it under a basket, but on a lampstand, and it gives light to all who are in the house. Let your light so shine before men..."*

Since this light is from God, and not of ourselves, it contains both the gentle and the firm. It contains both that which makes peace and that which makes war, as does God's own nature from which this light emanates. The Church will confront darkness as easily and automatically as the light from a lampstand, in a manner of speaking, confronts the darkness of a lightless room.

Some in our world have chosen to serve the darkness in this present age. The darkness exhibited by these individuals contends with the light expressed by people who are obedient to God's requirement of public witness. This attack on the light that is shining will take such forms as name calling, false accusations, revilement, and even physical abuse. The clash cannot be avoided in this present age; it will happen wherever the true light is shining. John the Baptist knew this when he confronted Herod. Jesus taught His disciples what to expect when He said in Matthew 10:24-25:

> A disciple is not above his teacher, nor a servant above his master. It is enough for a disciple that he be like his teacher, and a servant like his master. *If they have called the master of the house Beelzebub, how much more will they call those of his household!*

What then is to be our reaction when we are called all manner of names? First we must understand that we *will* be called names, as Jesus and John were, if we shine light into the world. Verse 26 says, *"Therefore do not fear them..."* This is to be our response. We should never turn down the light to avoid causing discomfort to evildoers; nor should we turn down the light to avoid disturbing the darkness as it corrupts millions of souls, preparing them for an eternity separated from God. However, turning down the light or purposefully keeping the light with which they are entrusted from shining into certain rooms of the house seems to be the natural tendency of most Christians and spiritual leaders at this present time. But under God's authority, a servant is not above his master. Verses 27 and 28 go on to say:

> Whatever I tell you in the dark, *speak in the light*; and what you hear in the ear, *preach on the housetops*. And do not fear those who kill the body but cannot kill the soul. But rather fear Him who is able to destroy both soul and body in hell.

Jesus is saying that our presentation of God, of all that He is, including His holiness, His sovereignty over His creation and the claims of His Messiah are to be publicly presented, even if it disturbs those who are actively working against that truth. Even if they label us, falsely accuse us or physically abuse us, the full presentation is to continue because God knows this is the strategy which will, if implemented, produce the maximum number of souls coming to repentance.

Salt seasons, light shines. Both actions are confrontational to people who have chosen to resist being flavored or illuminated. The only way to avoid any confrontation is to be neither salt nor light. From the perspective of what can be attained by a human being in this earthly life, aside from Jesus, John the Baptist demonstrated the highest grade of salt and the purest light. John's evident concern in this life was to please the Father and to fulfill His will. And yet at the time of his ministry, John was still under the authority and covering of the Old Covenant. The New Covenant and "the law of the Spirit of life in Christ Jesus (Romans 8:2)," the reign and rule of Grace, was not yet in force because Jesus had not yet died, risen from the dead, or ascended into Heaven.

Thus, John the Baptist was the last of the Old Testament prophets. (Jesus said in Matthew 11:14, that he came as Elijah). Our Lord seems to stress John's Old Testament status when He says in Matthew 11:13: "For all the prophets and the law prophesied until John." Jesus' ministry was the actual point of transition from the Old to the New Covenant. John's prophetic ministry was to prepare the way of the Messiah, whose ministry then brought the transition. (See also John 3:30)

This situation did not alter the fact that in the Kingdom of Heaven, John like all who serve God, was an ambassador to this earth, representing all that God is to all of the world. He had to fulfill his duty to be salt and light. This responsibility is what compelled John to rebuke King Herod regarding morality. King Herod was a Roman Tetrarch, a regional ruler or minor king in the Roman Empire. He was not even a Jew, but an Edomite and a pagan.

Was John wrong in holding King Herod accountable to God's moral standard? No, because everyone is accountable to God's moral standard; even an atheist; even satan. Was Herod answerable to God? Yes, of course! As we have already established, all of existence is accountable to God and, therefore, answerable to His holiness. At its most basic level, sin is "falling short of the glory of God" (Romans 3:23). So the personal beliefs of an individual do not in any way alter his accountability to God. Therefore, John correctly held King Herod to the moral standard that rules all of God's creation. He was salt and light to King Herod. But people who do not want their immorality exposed often respond harshly, and so King Herod used his authority to arrest John. Mark 6:17-18 (NIV) tells what happened: "For Herod himself had given orders to have John arrested, and he had him bound and put in prison ... For John had been saying to Herod, 'It is not lawful for you to have your brother's wife.' Not only had John been openly rebuking Herod about taking his brother's wife, but Luke 3:19 (NIV) adds this phrase regarding the subject matter of John's rebuke to king Herod: "...and all the other evil things he had done." Mark 6:19 (NIV) tells how Herod's brother's wife, Herodias, "...nursed a grudge against John and wanted to kill him..."

This episode, extending from the rebuke which led to John's arrest through his imprisonment, was a significant period of time. In the Amplified Bible, Luke 3:19-20 reads:

> But Herod the tetrach, who had been (repeatedly) told his fault and reproved with rebuke producing conviction, by John for [having] Herodias, his brother's wife, and for all the wicked things that Herod had done, added this to them all, that he shut up John in prison.

Even when John was in prison, Mark 6:20 says that for a while, Herod feared John and desired to listen to him. For that period of time he "protected" John or "kept him safe" (depending on the translation) from Herodias, who wanted him dead.

Was John fulfilling the will of God in publicly challenging a government official over a moral issue? Yes, of course, because as we have seen, civil authority, indeed *all* authority, is from God. King Herod was in a position to exercise the authority, delegated by God, to run civil government. He was doing so in a manner which was not compatible with the absolute moral standards that God has established both in the physical and in the spiritual realm.

God's representative, acting as salt and light, is required to hold those who exercise God's delegated authority accountable to God's basic understanding of good and evil (see Romans 13:3-4). This is what John the Baptist was doing.

We must remember that Jesus was on the earth at the time of these events. In fact Scripture records Christ's response to the news of John's arrest and imprisonment. In Mark 17:3 it says:

> And turning to His disciples He said, "See, I told you that Christians are not to be involved in politics. There is a wall of separation between Church and State!"

What?! I hope the reader isn't turning to the seventeenth chapter of St. Mark. Not only are there just sixteen chapters, but there is no such statement by Jesus or the Holy Spirit anywhere in the Scriptures. *The way some act and preach, however, you would think there was.*

There *is* a Holy Spirit-inspired statement that Jesus made regarding John, after he had been arrested and put into prison. Matthew 11:7-11 says:

> As they departed, Jesus began to say to the multitudes concerning John: "What did you go out to the wilderness to see? A reed shaken by the wind? But what did you go out to see? A man clothed in soft garments? Indeed, those who wear soft clothing are in kings' houses. But what did you go out to see? A prophet? Yes, I say to you, and *more than a prophet.* For this is He of whom it is written: 'Behold, I send my messenger before your face, who will prepare your way before you.' *Assuredly, I say to you, among those born of women there has not risen one greater than John the Baptist....*"

Instead of rebuking John for doing something that many modern-day pastors would have condemned as unbiblical, unloving or unkind, Jesus, knowing the whole story (John had sent two of his disciples to Christ from his prison cell), gave John the greatest statement of personal approval recorded in scripture regarding anyone except Himself. *"None greater,"* Jesus said. Why? Because John was a man of God — twenty-four hours a day, seven days a week, fifty-two weeks a year. *He was God's man all the time, wherever he happened to be, in every situation, regardless of the circumstances, no matter how high the cost to himself.* He was a representative of God; he was God's salt and light upon the earth. Although subject to human weaknesses, just as we all are, he was only, completely and always a man of God. And Jesus acknowledged him as such.

Remember, this man John was a prophet sent by God specifically to prepare the way for Jesus Himself. This man personally baptized Jesus in water and was there when the Holy Spirit descended from Heaven and rested upon Jesus. This was the man who identified Jesus as the Christ and was there when God spoke from Heaven saying, *"...this is My beloved Son, in whom I am well pleased." This same man, John the Baptist, had been arrested* **and** *imprisoned and was eventually to be beheaded, for calling into* *account the moral actions of a pagan government official.* Instead of warning His disciples that John had made a mistake to get involved in politics, Jesus gave him the greatest of compliments.

If John was out of line in holding Herod to account, here was the perfect opportunity, a situation created by His own prophet, for Jesus to have said so. Our Lord did not tell His disciples, or the multitudes, nor is He telling us today, that John should have behaved otherwise, that he should have focused only on the ministry of announcing the Messiah — because John's rebuke of Herod *was ministry also*. It was the ministry of acting as salt and light to the world!

Our Lord did not say to His disciples or to the multitudes, nor is He saying to us today that nothing should be done about the condition of our nation and government, except praying and evangelizing. By the same token, imagine the absurdity of saying that the effort one puts into being a good husband, wife, father or mother is wrongly spent, since it detracts from one's efforts in prayer and evangelism. That would be recognized, rightfully so, as utter nonsense! So also is the other statement. Nothing that the Lord requires of us is to be neglected, and He clearly requires us to be salt and light.

Nor are any of the things He requires of us mutually exclusive. We can pray and still be salt and light. Being salt and light is a fundamental element of evangelism. Being salt and light is essential to discipling the nations. It is even essential to the message of salvation. If we do not tell the sinner that he is under the authority of God and accountable to His holiness, of what shall he be convicted? And if he is not convicted, how shall he repent of his sins in order to find forgiveness and salvation? Jesus knew that John's public stand against Herod's wickedness was an important witness to the people. Therefore, why would He correct him when John was being exactly what God wanted him to be — even if that obedience cost him his life? So instead of a rebuke, Jesus gave him what he deserved, undoubtedly the greatest compliment recorded in scripture.

In the Kingdom of God, with an eye toward eternity, it is more important to publicly stand for righteousness than it is to live. That is the worth placed on being salt and light.

In all respects, John best epitomized the complete man of God. This is the man of whom his Lord said, "He was the burning and shining lamp" (John 5:35). He not only fulfilled his personal ministry and call, but he was salt and light to the earth — *even unto death.*

Chapter 5

The Sword of the Lord

Jesus said in Matthew 10:34:

*"Do not think that I came to bring peace on earth. I did not come to bring peace **but a sword**."*

Some do not acknowledge, and many are not even aware of, the spiritual truth contained in this scripture. Yet, there is a fundamental Christian principle expressed in these sobering but powerful words. The truth contained therein is foundational to the mandate of the Church, the spreading of the gospel and the ministry of the Holy Spirit within this present age.

When Jesus came to earth as the Messiah, He brought this sword with Him. The fact that our Lord brought this sword is important to remember. For Jesus Himself is the one who said, "*I did not come to bring peace but a sword.*" One of the reasons that He left Heaven and came to the earth was to bring this sword with the purpose of affecting the inhabitants of the earth.

Without question, there are numerous scriptures which say that Jesus, as the Prince of Peace, brings peace, and He does; however, the enjoyment of that peace is contingent upon the submission of the individual to Christ, as both Lord and Savior. Within the parameters of that submission there is divine peace. But outside of that submission exists the conflict that is produced by this sword.

In the age in which we live, there is open warfare between light and darkness. The sword of the Lord is that aspect of Christianity whereby we, His people, engage the darkness that is attempting to engulf and enslave this earth. God and His holiness are in conflict with satan and his evil. *This is the war.*

The sword that Christ brought is designed by God to openly confront that darkness, to confront and expose sin. The sword of the Lord authorizes us and compels us to contest God's enemies wherever they attempt to establish themselves on this earth. The sword is designed by God to force the conflict — even polarize it — to make the difference between good and evil easy to be seen, understood and compared, to make the distinctions between right and wrong readily visible, simple to discern. There is no doubt that there is a conflict, and the sword is aggressive by nature. Matthew 10:35 & 36 read: "For I have come to set a man *against* his father, a daughter *against* her mother, and a daughter-in-law *against* her mother-in-law. And a man's *foes* will be those of his own household." That is conflict. And that is why many people just skip over this scripture, not realizing that they are leaving out of the Christian foundation an essential element that is vital to the ultimate fulfillment of God's plan.

As we saw in the last chapter, without the public demonstration of Biblical salt and light, the most compelling witness for Christ will be missing. It is the use of the sword of the Lord by His people that will guarantee the greatest witness possible, even though it is confrontational. Therefore, in many cases, it will produce persecution. *Believe me, I tell you the truth, it is the confronting of sin that turns some into foes.* It is the proclamation that the moral standard for God's creation is righteousness that causes some to become hostile. It is the preaching which declares that each one of us will have to stand before God and give an account for every thought, word and deed that turns some into enemies.

The Greek word for "foes" in Matthew 10:36 is "echthros" which can also be translated "enemy." Vine's Expository Dictionary of New Testament Words says this about the word "foes:"

> Primarily denoting hatred or hateful (akin to *ecthos*, hate; perhaps associated with *ektos*, outside.) Hence, in the active sense, denotes hating, hostile; it is used as a noun signifying an enemy, adversary...

When the Word of God (the truth, the kingdom or the gospel) is presented in the manner Christ established and is led of the Holy Spirit, there will be some who react hatefully. That is because the sword that Jesus brought confronts all people regarding the realities and ramifications of sin.

There will be some who name the name of Christ who will be turned off by this truth, and there will be many who say it is destructive. However, please keep in mind as we study this further, that the author of this book did not bring the sword to this earth. Jesus did. I'm simply saying that if we want to please God, we must use the sword He has provided and in the manner He prescribed.

The sword does not negate or diminish the opportunity that every soul has to find grace. But those who are inclined to refuse that grace are forced to choose between the two spiritual realities involved in the conflict at the most elementary level. The sword of the Lord will force them to choose either God or satan. If the end result is negative for some, it will be so by their own choice, despite their being confronted by the sword of the Lord.

This conflict is seen clearly in the account in Luke 12:49-53 (parallel to Matthew 10) in which Jesus said:

> I came to send *fire* on the earth, and how I wish it were already kindled! But I have a baptism to be baptized with, and how distressed I am till it is accomplished! Do you suppose that I came to give peace on earth? I tell you, *not at all, but rather division.* For from *now on* five in one house will be *divided*: three against two, and two against three. Father will be divided against son and son against father, mother against daughter and daughter against mother, mother-in law against her daughter-in-law and daughter-in-law against her mother-in-law.

This is part of *Christ's* ministry for the earth. The sword that Jesus brought is a ministry that challenges, it is a ministry of confrontation. This absolutely essential confrontation is created by the fact that Jesus is the Christ, and without the atonement of His shed blood, we will die in our sins. It is a confrontation produced by moral light encountering immoral darkness.

At the same time, this sword of confrontation is not a license for meanness or for a lack of wisdom. This confrontational temperament is not a cloak for an un-Christ-like character. It is not freedom from self-control or kindness. Kindness and self-control are mandatory in the Kingdom of God. Bitterness, arrogance or a contentious spirit will remain sin, even if one understands and has implemented the godly principles of Christian warfare. At the same time and of equal importance, it is equally wrong for the timid Christian to use kindness and gentleness as a cloak to hide fear, apathy, cowardice and a willingness to tolerate open sin. Both extremes are wrong and very destructive to the Kingdom of God. The sword of the Lord is mandatory, and remains vital to God's plan. Confrontation with sin, evil and darkness remains God's specific purpose and mission for this sword.

I believe this sword has at least two major expressions and that it incorporates a third. Firstly, I believe that the sword of Matthew 10 is the same sword spoken of in Revelation 1:16 which, speaking of Jesus, says:

> He had in His right hand seven stars, *out of His mouth went a sharp two-edged sword*, and His countenance was like the sun shining in its strength.

Chapter 19:15, also speaking of Jesus, says:

> *Now out of His mouth goes a sharp sword, that with it He should strike the nations.* And He Himself will rule them with a rod of iron. He Himself treads the winepress of the fierceness and wrath of Almighty God.

The reason I emphasized the phrase "out of His mouth" in relationship to the sword is because Verse 13 says, "... *His* name is called *The Word of God.*" The sword is identified as that which proceeds out of His mouth, meaning His Word.

Referring again to Jesus, Revelation 2:12 says, "And to the angel of the church in Pergamos write, these things says He who has *the sharp two-edged sword....*" And verse 16 says, "Repent, or else I will come to you quickly and will *fight against* them with the sword *of my mouth.*" It is clear that this sword is a sword of confrontation. It is an aspect or side of Christianity that is inherently aggressive. The phrases *"strike the nations"* and *"fight against"* are terms of conflict and war. It is a sword meant for on-the-offensive confrontation.

The sword that Christ brought (referred to in Matthew 10:34) was Himself, as the Word of God. Thus the sword is that which proceeds out of His mouth — His Word — for He is the Word of God. According to John 1:1, "In the beginning was the Word, and the Word was with God, and the Word was God." As the Word, it must, of necessity, incorporate all that He has actually said, and it must succeed in all that God the Father sent forth His Word to accomplish.

When Jesus took on physical form, He remained God's Word, nevertheless. According to John 1:14, "...the Word became flesh and dwelt among us...." His personhood, His divine position in the Godhead as the Word of God, was not set aside when He became a man, and cannot be separated from Him just because He took on human form. In fact the Word of God actually "became flesh" in Jesus. The reality of this truth is seen clearly in I John 1:1, for in seeing, hearing and touching the man Jesus, the Holy Spirit says, they also saw, heard and touched the *"Word of Life."*

The sword is the Word of God, and the Word of God is Jesus, and Jesus is the Christ. Therefore, His mission as the Christ, the Messiah, cannot be separated from His position in the Godhead as the Word. It is who He is (the Word of God, the Son of God, God's light, righteousness, truth and judgment) that will divide good from evil; right from wrong; light from darkness; life from death. Subsequently, the confrontation produced by His light shining on ungodliness causes these divisions, these moral distinctions, thus even making "a man's foes ... those of his own household" (Matthew 10:36). In this scripture one cannot ignore the obvious fact that the work of this sword upon the earth even has preeminence over the relationships of family, upon which God places the highest importance. The reality that Jesus is the Christ - the Living Word of the One True God - is the reality which confronts people, as it must. If this particular confrontation does not occur, then the Gospel as delivered by Jesus is not being preached, because Jesus as the Word of God is the primary expression of the sword.

The second expression of the sword rests in the fact that this is the age of the Holy Spirit. Within the plan of God, after Christ's ascension into Heaven, Jesus sent the Holy Spirit to take His place on the earth (John 14:16-18) so the disciples (including you and me: see John 17:20), would not be left as orphans. The Holy Spirit was then to share the things of Christ with us (John 16:13-15).

Therefore, considering that the sword which Jesus brought represents a fundamental principle, foundational to the Faith, and realizing that the Holy Spirit now ministers the things of Christ to us, it naturally follows that Paul directs us, in Ephesians 6:17, to "...take up the helmet of salvation, and the *sword of the Spirit, which is the Word of God.*" This is the same sword which Jesus brought to the earth because it is identified as the Word of God. The Holy Spirit continues the ministry of the sword, and also confronts darkness and challenges individuals to repent of their sins, which is the ministry of the sword. This confronting of sin is substantiated by Jesus in John 16:7-11 when He says this about the Holy Spirit:

> Nevertheless I tell you the truth. It is to your advantage that I go away; for if I do not go away, the Helper will not come to you; but if I depart, I will send Him to you. And *when He has come, He will convict the world of sin, and of righteousness, and of judgment*: of sin, because they do not believe in *Me;* of righteousness, because *I go to my Father,* and you see me no more; of judgment, because the ruler of this world is judged.

The Holy Spirit takes the sword which Jesus set into motion as a part of His own ministry and continues that ministry on behalf of

Christ on the earth.

This is an age of conflict, the conflict between good and evil, between the Kingdom of God and the kingdom of satan. The only way to avoid this conflict is to do *nothing* that God requires with regard to the sword, or to do *something*, but to do it in a manner contrary to Christ's will and to the leading of the Holy Spirit. The fact that the sword of the Lord is going to turn some into enemies is inevitable. His sword, which is the Word of God, will always have that effect on some. This is seen clearly in II Corinthians 2:14-17, which says,

> Now thanks be to God who always leads us in triumph in Christ, and through us diffuses the fragrance *of His knowledge* in every place. For we are to God the *fragrance of Christ* among those who are being saved and *among those who are perishing. To the one we are the aroma of death leading to death*, and to the other the aroma of life leading to life. And who is sufficient for these things? For we are not, as so many, peddling *the Word of God* (Author's note: Remember that the Word is the sword of the Lord); but as of sincerity, but as from God, *we speak in the sight of God in Christ.*

The Holy Spirit makes this sobering statement in verse 17: "For we are not, *as so many*, peddling the Word of God...." The word "peddling" in the Greek is "Kapeleuo," which could be translated "corrupt," "huckster" or "hawking," or "adulterate." In context, the word "peddling" stands out in contrast to the idea of being "the fragrance of Christ." The fragrance of Christ has a predetermined aroma which to some is death and to some is life. The fragrance of Christ will always be so, without exception, because it is the sword, the Word of God (Verse 17). When presented properly as the sword, it is also the fragrance of Christ, and it will have a specific aroma that will produce specific results. When peddled, it ceases to be the sword. When peddled, it ceases to be the Word of God. When peddled, it is no longer the fragrance of Christ. Thus, to those who are perishing, the divine aroma, when peddled, ceases to mean death, because it ceases to confront sin.

The Apostles were not peddlers. They carried and used the sword of the Spirit. They were in deed, in truth, and in every respect, the fragrance of Christ. Verse 17 says: "For we are not, as so many, peddling the word of God; but as of *sincerity,* but as *from God,* we speak in the sight *of God in Christ."*

The words, "sincerity, ... *from God,* ... *in the sight of God in Christ,"* are all indicators and evidence in our life and ministry of whether or not we indeed have the fragrance of Christ. If we are sincere in our handling of the Word of God, there will be a specific fragrance. There will be a divine aroma of Christ in which God will be well pleased. But to those who are perishing that divine fragrance convicts of death. This cannot be helped because the choice they have made for their lives contradicts and defies the holiness and righteousness of God.

The sword of the Lord, to those who choose darkness, will always reveal that their eternal decision was to reject light. That decision, until repented of, will transform most of them into foes, hostile to those who carry the sword of the Spirit in their hand.

Were the Apostles the fragrance of Christ? Did they manifest the aroma that was pleasing to God? Did they properly take up and use the sword of the Spirit? There is one sure piece of evidence in answering these questions — did they have the type of foes that Jesus refers to? Were they persecuted for righteousness' sake?

The correct presentation of Christ is an aroma of death to those who have given themselves to lawlessness in an affront to God's will and holiness (again, it will always be so in this age) because the sword convicts of sin, righteousness and judgment. In that conflict there is no peace. That is why Jesus said, "Do not think that I came to bring peace..."

That is the conflict of this age, and that is the objective of the sword of the Lord. Light impacting darkness. Good encountering evil. God offering mankind a way to avoid eternal separation from Himself. However, some will be offended by the offer, if the offer is made in the way God wants it made, that is, in a manner that convicts of sin, righteousness and judgment. If those three are not properly presented and dealt with, salvation will not even be realized, let alone secure. For a person must be saved from sin because of His righteousness, in order to avoid judgment. That is salvation and that is why the Holy Spirit convicts in these three areas.

This brings us to the third expression to be considered. 1) Jesus brought a sword, and that sword is Himself; the Word of God. 2) The Holy Spirit continues the process established by Jesus in that He, Himself picks up and uses the same sword. 3) Both points, number one and two, are to work through His people - the Church, the Body of Christ.

Remember, in II Corinthians 2:14 it says, "... and *through us* diffuses the fragrance...." And verse 15 says, "For *we are* to God the fragrance...." And verse 16 says, " To the one *we* are not, as so many, peddling the Word of God; but as of sincerity, but as *from God, we speak* in the sight of God in Christ." If this ministry of the sword is established by Christ, ministered by the Holy Spirit for the earth, then it stands to reason and scripture that ministering the sword would also be a requirement of the Church.

If there is anyone who remains skeptical regarding Christians using this sword, then let me ask that one this question; Who is the individual who is supposed to "put on the whole armor of God" in Ephesians, chapter six? That same person is to take up *"the sword of the spirit"* as part of the armor. That person, as we all know, is each and every individual believer, forming, as a whole, the Body of Christ — the Church.

To avoid personal discomfort, many make every effort to ignore this side of the Gospel. But no matter how much one tries, the holiness of God that convicts of sin cannot be separated from the presentation of the Gospel which, if accepted, results in the forgiveness of that same sin. Circumventing the moral absolutes of God diminishes the gospel. If that happens, the Gospel is no longer the "power of God unto salvation" (Romans 1:16). When we shine the light, it automatically confronts darkness because of its nature and essence — all the time, in every situation — unless we turn out the light or alter it to the point that it no longer remains divine light.

The real problem with some in this world is that they do not want to do what is holy. In fact, they want to do as many unholy things as they can. At the same time we have a God who has given His people a mandate to "walk in the light as He is in the light." (I John 1:6) There will be confrontation — in fact, there had better be confrontation. If there isn't, it is because we are not walking in the light. There is no way around it, the sword of the Lord is a weapon for confrontation. Could anyone really think that foes are created by passivity, denial, apathy and non-confrontation? Indeed, light exposes sin. When manifest, it will always confront darkness. In fact, no extra effort is needed — just shine, and confrontation with darkness occurs.

As light has always been a state of being, so also is darkness, because of satan's action. There are those who desire to walk in darkness, and for this reason they become foes to the Light. Jesus confirms this in John 3:18-20:

> He who believes in Him is not condemned; but he who does not believe is condemned already, because he has not believed in the name of the only begotten Son of God. And *this is the condemnation, that light has come into the world,* (Author's note: "I have not come to bring peace but a sword") *and men loved darkness rather than light, because their deeds were evil. For everyone practicing evil hates the light* (Author's note: "A man's foes will be those of his own household.") and does not come to the light, lest his *deeds should be exposed.*

Light automatically confronts darkness, and light has come into the world as a sword. This divine confrontation will occur in all cases unless, against God's will, we purposefully hide or turn down the light. When the light is dimmed, what does the darkness do? It increases in intensity in direct proportion to the degree of dimness that has occurred. That is exactly what we see going on in our present day. As Christians by the tens of thousands have turned down their light, darkness has exploded. In a cosmic-level struggle between light and darkness which has spanned multiple epic time periods and ages, eternally affecting both the physical and the spiritual realms, could we expect it to be any different? Could we seriously think that our life-span so outweighs the eternal ramifications of this struggle that God would call an intermission? And that satan would agree not to enslave another soul so that we could watch our soap operas or build our own little fellowships above and beyond the reach of this struggle? Remember Jesus said: "He who is not with Me is against Me, and he who does not gather with Me scatters." (Luke 11:23) And Jesus brought a sword. Confrontation with darkness is standard operating procedure for this age, because in this age evil is an open contestant desiring to displace the Almighty and dominate existence.

This is an age of conflict; however, this truth is ignored by the vast majority of people of goodwill. This ignorance, or denial, hands the adversary a major advantage in the outworking of the conflict. Those who believe in God, and in His Son, Jesus Christ, must wake up. This is an age of conflict. We are not called to a life of ease, to stockpile goods for personal security and comfort. We are called to engage the enemy, to contest him and his philosophy, to challenge his sway over the souls of our fellow human beings, to shine light into darkness, to bring truth to bear on lies, to be ambassadors of Christ in the midst of a crooked and perverse generation.

In this conflict, God requires us to have a warrior's attitude and demeanor. II Timothy 2:3-4 says, "You therefore must endure hardships as a *good soldier* of Jesus Christ. No one engaged in *warfare* entangles himself with the affairs of this life, that he may please him who *enlisted him as a soldier.*"

Isn't it strange that there are those today who are afraid of military terms? Yet if we walk in a manner pleasing to God, we are enlisted and "engaged in warfare." The scripture says we "must endure hardships," which are not the normal ups and downs of life, nor even the trials and testing of our discipleship walk with the Holy Spirit. Instead they are hardships suffered for being "a good soldier of Jesus Christ." The hardships are produced as a result of our personal military activities in God's army. I would hazard a guess that Christ has many churchgoers, but very few soldiers. How important is this tour of duty, this enlistment? Again the scripture says, *"No one* engaged in warfare entangles himself in the affairs of this life...." Why? "...that he may please *Him* who enlisted him."

We should be concerned about this life only to the degree necessary to fulfill God's required responsibilities to our families and neighbors. Everything else is to be focused on the war. Even our families, as in a human physical war, are to focus on winning the conflict. Now this does not mean that we should not take time for R&R (military term for rest and relaxation), but the times of fun are not the focus. "...Pleasing Him who enlisted us" is. Is there a desire on our part that we "please him who enlisted" us? We are specifically instructed not to become entangled in the "affairs of this life," in order to remain focused on the warfare. That's how important this is. But is it really warfare? Yes, it is warfare. II Corinthians 10:4-5 says:

> "For the *weapons of our warfare* are not carnal but *mighty in God for pulling down strongholds, casting down arguments* and *every high thing that exalts itself against the knowledge of God, bringing every thought into captivity to the obedience of Christ ....*"

The fact that the weapons are not carnal does not alter the fact that they are weapons, nevertheless, to be used for the purpose of warfare.

The spiritual dimension of the conflict is very real, but the public application has been ignored or overlooked. So before we continue let us look at the scripture that many use to suggest that there is only one side, the spiritual side, to the conflict. Ephesians 6:12 reads: "For we do not wrestle against flesh and blood, but against principalities, against powers, against the rulers of the darkness of this age, against spiritual hosts of wickedness in the heavenly places." I believe this is not stated in an "either/or" manner but, instead, that it refers to something additional. For example, The Amplified Bible reads this way: "For we are not wrestling with flesh and blood — contending *only* with physical opponents — but against...." The Williams New Testament reads: "For our contest is not with human foes *alone*...." I believe the baseline truth in this scripture, concerns the ultimate conflict between God and satan; therefore, the ultimate conflict is in the spiritual realm. But this does not mean that the physical realm is not also a part of the battlefield; in fact, for this age it is the main part of the battlefield. For satan from his very first act after the Creation, and up to the present, has attempted and continues to attempt to take absolute control and authority over the physical realm. His final desperate act will be to physically possess the antichrist.

Although the outcome of the ultimate conflict will be decided in the spiritual realm, the struggle includes who is going to control the creation. The spiritual battle is also being fought out in the physical realm. Let me give you a very clear example from the scripture. Look at Acts 19:11-16, which reads:

> Now God worked unusual miracles by the hands of Paul, so that even handkerchiefs or aprons were brought from his body to the sick, and the diseases left them and the evil spirits went out of them. Then some of the itinerant Jewish exorcists took it upon themselves to call the name of the Lord Jesus over those who had evil spirits, saying, "We exorcise you by the Jesus whom Paul preaches." Also there were seven sons of Sceva, a Jewish chief priest, who did so. And the evil spirit answered and said, "Jesus I know, and Paul I know; but who are you?" Then the man in whom the evil spirit was leaped on them, overpowered them, and prevailed against them, so that they fled out of that house naked and wounded.

This scripture is a clear example of the battle in the spiritual realm being played out on the stage of the physical. Specifically, verse 16 relates the incident in which the demon-possessed individual jumped on the seven men and beat them up to the point that they were wounded and stripped naked. Now, it seems to me that being wounded might indicate the presence of some *blood* and that being naked would definitely reveal *flesh,* so that *this* wrestling was at least with *flesh and blood*. Clearly, Ephesians 6:12 does not mean that there is no confrontation with humanity — but that the ultimate struggle is with satan and his demonic structure. Yet that struggle does play out in the physical arena. Another example is I Timothy 4:1-5 which says:

> Now the Spirit expressly says that in latter times some will depart from the faith, giving heed to deceiving spirits and doctrines of demons, speaking lies in hypocrisy, having their own conscience seared with a hot iron, forbidding to marry, and commanding to abstain from foods which God created to be received with thanksgiving by those who believe and know the truth. For every creature of God is good, and nothing is to be refused if it is received with thanksgiving; for it is sanctified by the word of God and prayer.

Again we encounter the spiritual entering the physical. We see the conflict of darkness warring with light. In this particular time period, "some" departed "from the faith;" hence, the darkness prevailed because they ("some" in the physical realm) gave "heed to deceiving spirits and doctrines of demons...." Who is speaking the "lies in hypocrisy?" It is men in the physical realm giving heed to demons from the spiritual.

The NIV translates verse 2 this way: "Such teachings come *through* hypocritical liars...." The Phillips Modern English Translation reads: "teachings *given by men* who are lying hypocrites...." The NAS reads: "*by means* of the hypocrisy of liars...." And The Twentieth Century New Testament translates: "who will *make use* of the hypocrisy of lying teachers...." In this present age the battle is being fought out in the physical realm by spiritual forces, both good and evil. Both of the teachings specifically cited in I Timothy 4:3, that were received from demons and presented through men, deal with physical matters — marriage and food.

Another example is in Revelation 18:1-3:

> After these things I saw another angel coming down from heaven, having great authority, and the earth was illuminated with his glory. And he cried mightily with a loud voice, saying, "Babylon the great is fallen, is fallen, and has become a *dwelling place of demons, a prison for every foul spirit*, and a cage for every unclean and hated bird! For *all the nations* have drunk of the wine of the wrath of her fornication, *the kings of the earth* have committed fornication with her, and *the merchants of the earth* have become rich through the abundance of her luxury."

The sphere influenced or affected is the nations and the earth — the physical. Kings and merchants are flesh and blood, just as men speaking lies in hypocrisy. Although the fact remains that the physical is being influenced in these particular situations by the demonic from the spiritual realm, the physical is most definitely involved.

With this scriptural understanding, let us go back now to II Corinthians 10:4-5, concerning the weapons of our warfare. These weapons, though not carnal, are nevertheless used in the physical realm against physical targets. To see this more clearly, we need only look at the context of the Apostle's statement. Beginning with verses one and two, we read:

> Now I, Paul, myself am pleading with you by the meekness and gentleness of Christ — who in presence am lowly among you, but being absent am bold toward you. But I beg you that when I am present I may not be bold *with that confidence by which I intend to be bold against some*, who think of us as if we walked *according to the flesh*.

There are several key statements and phrases here that continue to give us understanding of verses 4 and 5. First notice that the basis of Paul's intended action is a certain confidence "by which" he was going to take that action. Also remember that he said, "...I beg you that when I am present I may not also be bold...." His desire was that when he returned to the church at Corinth he would not have to take this certain posture towards the whole church. But he would have if light had demanded it! He had the confidence and he had already made up his mind that he intended "to be bold towards *some*". I believe that "confidence" was his authority in Christ (mentioned in verse eight) and the obvious "power of Christ" (in II Corinthians 12:9) that rested on him. His desire was not to have to turn this confidence loose on them, but he was going to focus it on "some" who were participating in the ongoing activities of the Corinthian church. These "some" were hindering the work there, accusing Paul and the others of walking in the flesh, for II Corinthians 10:2 said: "who think of us as if we walked in the flesh." In this context Paul says in verse 3, "For though we walk in the flesh *we do not war according to the flesh.*"

Remember the scriptures in II Timothy on being enlisted by God to conduct warfare. Here in II Corinthians the Apostle again states clearly this Christian expression of war. In this instance, it is clear that the object of this Christian expression of war was the group of troublemakers attending the church at Corinth. This upcoming action of "confidence," the intention "to be bold against some," is described as an expression of war. The target is "flesh and blood" in the physical realm! But the Apostle also recognizes the ultimate source of motivation influencing these troublemakers, for, in II Corinthians 11:13-15 he says, about these same individuals:

> For such are false apostles, deceitful workers, transforming themselves into apostles of Christ. And no wonder! For Satan himself transforms himself into an angel of light. Therefore it is no great thing if his ministers also transform themselves into ministers of righteousness, whose end will be according to their works.

Therefore, I conclude that although the initial source and motivation of a conflict may be in the spiritual realm, this does not mean that the point or vehicle of expression within the physical realm will escape the confrontation of Christian warfare. For the Apostle had just made those troublemakers his targets in the ongoing war between light and darkness.

In this epic struggle between good and evil, there are always physical targets of Christian warfare, just as when John the Baptist engaged Herod in warfare, and just as when the Apostle Paul waged war on "some" from the Corinthian church. This activity is none other than the function of being salt and light. This activity is also a specific aspect of the ministry of the sword. It is Christian warfare, and God Himself has enlisted every Christian as a combatant, "For the *weapons* of <u>our</u> *warfare* are not carnal but *mighty in God....*" Though they were accused of walking in the flesh, their defense was that the activities of their ministry were not motivated by, or based upon, the flesh. The Apostle's confidence to engage in this Christian warfare came from his desire to present Christ to them, the Corinthian church, and them to Christ. This was in complete compliance with the heavenly rules of engagement. For the weapons of warfare that are mighty in God are "for pulling down strongholds, casting down arguments and *every* high thing that *exalts itself against the knowledge of God*, bringing *every* thought into captivity *to the obedience <u>of Christ</u>.*"

Look at this passage in II Corinthians 10:4-5 from the Message paraphrase:

> The world is unprincipled. It's dog eat dog out there! The world doesn't fight fair. But we don't live or fight our battles that way — never have and never will. The tools of our trade aren't for marketing or manipulation, *but they are for demolishing that entire massively corrupt culture.* We use our powerful God-tools for *smashing* warped philosophies, *tearing down* barriers erected against the truth of God, fitting every loose thought and emotion and impulse into the structure of life shaped by Christ.

Take special notice of Paul's attitude. It is the disposition of a warrior. No matter where the stronghold, whether spiritual or physical, if its strength resulted from exalting itself against the knowledge of God, Paul engaged in Christian warfare in order to pull it down. No matter where an argument was made, whether in the church at Corinth or elsewhere, if it exalted itself against the knowledge of God, Paul sought to cast it down by engaging in Christian warfare. The Apostle took on a military posture toward anything and every concept that lifted itself up against the truth of the existence and sovereignty of God Almighty, for the purpose of bringing every thought into obedience to Christ. Why? Because he was enlisted by God to fight in an eternal war between the Sovereign he served and the prince of darkness.

The battle rages, even as you read these pages, on behalf of each and every soul. Paul understood the war and the tactics of the enemy. *He knew that every teaching, concept, policy or program that could keep a soul from his Creator must be challenged so that as many as possible would be kept from deception.* Secondarily, at the coming of Jesus to earth, God set in motion His eternal plan. That plan is stated in Ephesians 1:9-10:

> [H]aving made known to us the *mystery of His will*, according to His good pleasure which He purposed in Himself, that in the dispensation of the fullness of times *He* might gather together in one *all things in Christ, both* which are in heaven *and which are on earth — in Him.*

That plan was set into motion at the moment John the Baptist began to *publicly* point to Jesus. Obviously, the plan was known from the foundations of the world, but man's obligation to be obedient to it was now required. We are required to bring the earth into Christ throughout this entire age. The concept of the sword and Christian warfare was also implemented at the same moment in time, with God Himself already at war. For Hebrews 1:13 says, "But to which of the angels has He ever said: 'Sit at my right hand, till *I make your enemies* your footstool?'"

God is already active in subduing the enemies of Christ because the eternal plan was implemented when Christ Jesus came to earth some two thousand years ago. As God has purposed to subdue the enemies of His Christ, He expects His people to have this same attitude. Phillipians 3:17-21 says:

> Brethren, join in following my example, and note those who so walk, as you have us for a pattern. For many walk, of whom I have told you often, and now tell you even weeping, that they are the enemies of the cross of Christ: whose end is destruction, whose god is their belly, and whose glory is in their shame — who set their mind on earthly things. For our citizenship is in heaven, from which we also eagerly wait for the Savior, the Lord Jesus Christ, who will transform our lowly body that it may be conformed to His glorious body, according to *the working* by which He is able even *to subdue* all things to Himself.

Notice that the Holy Spirit holds up the attitude and actions of the Apostle Paul as our example of how we should conduct ourselves in all things, including our relationship to our culture and the world. He adds that we should observe others who walk in this manner and that together they are to be our examples of conduct. They are contrasted to those (undoubtedly religious leaders) with worldly and fleshly priorities.

The reason I use this scripture is to point out again that God is active. Verse 21 says that the ultimate transformation of our bodies from flesh to spirit will be accomplished "according to the working by which He is able even to subdue all things to Himself." This "working" includes that divine involvement of which we speak. It obviously encompasses more than His involvement in the political affairs of the nations, but it definitely includes that aspect also. This "working" has been active since the beginning. But when Jesus took His seat next to the One True God, God Himself began to subdue all things, bringing them into Christ. The New Living Translation reads: "...using the same mighty power that He will use to conquer everything, everywhere." The word "subdue" in the Greek is "hupotasso," a military term meaning to cause to rank under something or someone, to put into subjection; thus to conquer, subject or subdue. As this passage confirms, the Godhead is already actively working to subdue the enemies of Christ. I Corinthians 15:20-28 says:

> But now Christ is risen from the dead, and has become the firstfruits of those who have fallen asleep. For since by man came death, by Man also came the resurrection of the dead, For as in Adam all die, even so *in Christ* all shall be made alive, But each one in his own order: Christ the firstfruits, afterward those who are Christ's at His coming. Then comes the end, when He delivers the kingdom to God the Father, *when He puts an end to all rule and all authority and power.* For He must reign till He has put all enemies under His feet. The last enemy that will be destroyed is death. For "He has put all things under His feet." But when He says "all things are put under Him," it is evident that He who put all things under Him is excepted. Now when all things are made subject to Him, then the Son Himself will also be subject to Him who put all things under Him, that God may be all in all.

In Adam, all die; but *in Christ*, all will live — this represents the most important and critical choice that mankind faces. Each person's eternity rests upon the decision either to stay in Adam or to be subdued by God and placed into Christ. At the core of salvation is the acceptance of Him as God. Without submission to Him as Almighty God, there is no redemption. If one does not accept Him as God, how then is forgiveness of sin obtained? Only God can forgive sin. If God does not exist, then there is no sin. But of course God does exist; therefore, the essential question will always be whether each person has submitted to Him as God. Because if we are submitting to Him as God, He will place us in Christ and place Christ in us.

Notice that the enemies of Christ range from independent or unsubmitted "rule ... authority and power," to death itself. All the enemies of the Kingdom of God will be put under the feet of Christ. Everything will be put under Christ; that is, everything except the One who is subduing all things, because His position in the Godhead is that of the Eternal Father, and as God the Father, He will always be *all in all*. This fact about God the Father is most fundamental. The creation then, in order to be in the right, must recognize Him as He is — *"all in all."*

Observe verse 28, which, speaking of Jesus, says, "all things are *made subject* to Him...." The New Living translation says, "when He has *conquered* all things...." The Message paraphrase reads, "When everything and everyone is finally under God's rule...." And the Amplified Bible says:

> However, when everything is *subjected* to Him, then the Son Himself will also subject Himself to [the Father] Who put all things under Him, so that God may be all in all — that is, be everything to everyone, supreme, the indwelling and controlling factor of life.

We cannot separate the holiness of God from the demands of the Gospel, nor can we separate the absolute sovereignty of God from that same Gospel. For upon these two considerations rest the entire purpose of God toward man. Through Scripture we see God's earthly involvement. For again, the Spirit says: "...then the Son Himself will also be subject to *him who put all things under* Him..." In the Old Testament, we have seen that God was obviously and completely involved in the affairs of men. However, in fulfillment of Psalm 110:1, God began the actual process of making the enemies of Christ His footstool after Jesus took His position of authority at His right hand. The Apostle Paul, whom the Holy Spirit has set up as the example by which we are to pattern our lives, was involved in fighting "every high thing that exalts itself against the knowledge of God" in every area of our culture. The reason? Colossians 1:28, speaking of Jesus, says, "Him we preach, warning every man and teaching every man in all wisdom, that we may *present every man perfect in Christ Jesus.*"

As we pointed out, this is the very motive and heart of God, the mystery of His will: to gather everything on earth and in Heaven into the life of His Son and under His authority. This is why Paul acted as he did. This is what drove him. Verse 29 says this about Paul's inner motive: "To this end I also labor, *striving according to His working which works in me mightily.*"

If God has a plan and is personally implementing that plan, reason and scripture dictate, that He also desires His people to participate with Him in its full implementation and completion. The Apostle Paul not only adopted an aggressive Gospel message, based on the fact that God has made Jesus Lord of all, but he also taught and trained others to be aggressive in the same way. The Holy Spirit calls this confrontational disposition "warfare"

Both the Apostle Paul and the early Church lived their lives in obedience to God's eternal plan to subdue the enemies of Christ because they understood God's will and, therefore, complied with His marching orders. The war was on and they had enlisted; therefore, they fought in obedience to God.

When these troublemakers who were negatively affecting the Corinthian church "exalted" themselves "against the knowledge of God" they showed themselves to be enemy targets — see again II Corinthians 11:13-15. The Apostle, as a good soldier of Jesus Christ, then began "pulling down" the stronghold they were building, and began "casting down" the argument they were making. It does not matter where the stronghold is. The source of the argument is irrelevant. The location of the "thing that exalts itself against the knowledge of God" does not matter — whether in the spiritual realm or upon the earth. If it attacks or is against the knowledge of God or His Christ, it becomes a target in the war.

Remember that the weapons referred to are not physical in that they are not tanks, guns, bullets or bombs. And though the weapons will have physical targets and they may be applied physically, they are, in and of themselves, nonphysical weapons. Depending on the circumstances, the weapons may range from kindness and charity to driving the money changers out of the temple, or standing up to the governmental Herod's of our day.

The targets also range across the whole spectrum of human and spiritual activity wherever there is a thought contrary to the plan of God. Obviously, we do not lack targets. And this was the example that the Apostle set. Look at Acts 17:16-23, which reads:

> Now while Paul waited for them at Athens, his spirit was provoked within him when he saw *that the city was given over to idols. Therefore* he reasoned in the synagogue with the Jews and with the Gentile worshipers, and in the marketplace daily with those who happened to be there. Then certain Epicurean and Stoic philosophers encountered him. And some said, "What does this babbler want to say?" Others said, "He seems to be a proclaimer of foreign gods," because he preached to them Jesus and the resurrection. And they took him and brought him to the Areopagus, saying, "May we know what this new doctrine is of which you speak? For you are bringing some strange things to our ears. Therefore we want to know what these things mean." For all the Athenians and the foreigners who were there spent their time in nothing else but either to tell or to hear some new thing. Then Paul stood in the midst of the Areopagus and said, "Men of Athens, I perceive that in all things you are very religious: for as I was passing through and considering the objects of your worship, I even found an altar with this inscription: TO THE UNKNOWN GOD. Therefore, the One whom you worship without knowing, Him I proclaim to you...."

Notice that Paul became aware that the city was given over to idols. Idol worship is contrary to the openly-expressed will of God. Once this awareness occurred, his spirit was "provoked within him" like a warrior sensing the nearness of the enemy and seeing a target come into view. Notice also that the target, this time, was not in the

Church but within a secular city that was given over to paganism. What if a city is given over to homosexuality? What if a city is given over to pornography? What if a country is given over to killing innocent human babies?

This is the premise of this book: The Christian viewpoint established by God and placed within the believer by the Holy Spirit is to deem the whole earth and everything in it accountable to God. Because the Apostle had this mindset, he *"therefore ...* reasoned *in the synagogue ... and in the marketplace* daily...." (verse 17). The secular realm, as we have seen in previous chapters of this book, is all under the authority of God and answerable and accountable to Him — now. Therefore the whole city (in this example, Athens), the complete community, is all a part of the battlefield upon which good and evil, God and satan, are at war. Paul acted in obvious accord with the truth he had been taught by God. For it is God's plan. It is not my plan nor is it Paul's, but it is apostolic and it is Biblical. Paul not only taught it, he lived it — as should we. The fact that pagans were doing what pagans do, when Paul arrived in Athens, did not put them outside the scope of God's authority. Nor did it remove them from the battlefield as a target of Christian warfare, even though the activity was outside the religious realm of the Synagogue. Paul simply took his weapons to the "marketplace" where the target was. It did not matter to Paul that the targets eventually became the great philosophies and philosophers of Greece. Nor did it matter that he was called names, when they said, "What does this babbler want to say...." Paul was concerned only with being a good soldier of Jesus Christ; therefore, he went to war. The end result of this engagement which Paul launched is written in Acts 17:34: "However, some men joined him and believed, among them Dionysius the Areopagite, a woman named Damaris, and others with them."

A.T. Robertson, in his work, Word Pictures in the New Testament, says this concerning Dionysius the Areopagite:

> One of the judges of the Court of Areopagus. That of itself was no small victory. He was one of this college of twelve judges who helped to make Ath-

ens famous. Eusebius says that he became afterwards bishop of the Church at Athens and died a martyr.

Also look at Acts 19:23-41, where the whole city of Ephesus rioted because the teachings of the way of Christ threatened the economics of the craftsmen who made idols for the temple of the goddess Diana.
It is a war, and there will be confrontations and battles if we are good soldiers of Jesus Christ. John 1:4-14 says.

> In Him was life, and *the life was the light* of men. *And the light shines in the darkness*, and the darkness did not comprehend it. There was a man sent from God, whose name was John. This man came for a witness, to bear witness of the Light, that all through Him might believe. He was not that Light, but was sent to bear witness of *that Light.* That was *the true Light* which gives light to every man coming into the world. He was in the world, and the world was made through Him, and the world did not know Him. He came to His own, and His own did not receive Him. But as many as received Him, to them He gave the right to become children of God, to those who believe in His name: who were born, not of blood, nor of the will of the flesh, nor of the will of man, but of God. *And the Word became flesh* and dwelt among us, and we beheld His glory, the glory as of the only begotten of the Father, full of grace and truth.

When the Scripture says, *"that* Light" (verse 8), it is referring to the divine Light that confronts darkness. Now, that *"true* Light" (verse 9) is also divine Life (verse 4). "the Life" is Jesus, "the Word" (verse 14) and the Word is the sword of the Lord. True light acts as a sword because it shines forth the properties of its source. In this case, the Source is Christ, the Word of God. Hebrews 4:12-13 says,

> For the *word of God is living and powerful, and sharper than any two-edged sword, piercing* even to the division of soul and spirit, and of joints and marrow, *and is a discerner of the thoughts and intents of the heart.* And there is no creature *hidden from His sight,* (author's note: divine light) *but all things are naked and open to the eyes of Him* to Whom we must give account.

The Greek word for "piercing" is "diikneomai" and it could also be translated as "cutting," "slicing" or "penetrating." The Word of God, described in this way, is a sword *sharper* than any physical two-edged sword; it cuts, penetrates or pierces deep into the individual — if it is *"the Word,"* if it is *"that Light,"* if it is *"living,"* if it is *"sincere."*

With this in mind, let us look at Ephesians 5:13: "But all things that are exposed are made *manifest by the light,* for *whatever* makes manifest *is* light."

No matter how we view the relationship of an object to the light shining upon it, of this we can be certain — it is light that exposes what is in the darkness. The Greek word for "expose" is "elegcho," and it means "to bring to light, expose, set forth, to convict, rebuke or reprove." Thayer's Greek-English Lexicon says, "by conviction to bring to light, to expose." God's light shines on everything, nothing escapes it. Hebrews says His Word pierces or penetrates to the point of the division between the soul and spirit within a man. Then, having cut to that point, the Word being living and powerful, has the ability to discern the very thoughts and intents of the heart. And because God is both truth and light, and because all things exist and are maintained by God who is their source, nothing is hidden from His sight. His light shines upon everything. Hebrews 4:13 says, "... *all things* are naked and open to the eyes of Him to whom we must give an account." In context, we continue to read in Ephesians 5:8-13:

> For you were once darkness, *but now you are light in the Lord. Walk as children of light* (for the fruit

of the Spirit is in all *goodness, righteousness, and truth), finding out* what is acceptable to the Lord. And have no fellowship with the unfruitful works of darkness, *but rather expose them*. For it is shameful even to speak of those things which are done by them in secret. But all things that are exposed are made manifest by the light, for whatever makes manifest is light.

At first glance, some would see a conflict between "expose them" and "shameful to even speak of those things," but the context of the chapter continues to give ample guidance. Obviously, speaking of different expressions of darkness as specific sins is not prohibited by the Holy Spirit or the Apostle since they have just done that very thing (verses 1-8), here as in dozens of other places throughout the Scripture. Nor does it prohibit what the Lord said to the woman at the well when He told her that the man she was with now was not her husband. Therefore, from the context, there cannot be something that limits our ability to expose wrongdoing since we have just been commanded by God to do that very thing. Indeed, as we have already seen, God Himself will fully expose the hidden things of darkness in each and every one of us.

Light exposing darkness for the purpose of Holy Spirit-led conviction and correction is godly, and though uncomfortable, it is not shameful, but clearly desirable in order that truth may prevail. However, any other purpose for talking about evil and vile actions, or about a person committing sin, *is* shameful. In fact, that type of talk is perhaps sin in and of itself — considered by God to be as evil as any other sin being talked about. For the Scriptures condemn a talebearer and a gossip as much as they condemn an adulterer and a thief. For just as the divine nature is such that it will expose the sin of the rebellious, the proud and the arrogant, it is equally committed to cover the confessed sin of the repentant, the humble and the meek — and so should we.

The exposing of sin is an action automatically produced by walking in the light. An example of talking about sin in order to expose it is seen when the Apostle Paul is dealing with the type of darkness referred to in Ephesians 5:12, when we read in I Corinthians 5:1: "It is actually reported that there is sexual immorality among you, *and such sexual immorality as is not even named among the Gentiles* — that a man has his father's wife!" He then goes on in verses two through eight to deal with that situation.

Principally, what is lacking in the Church at large, and among Christians in general, is the willingness and obedience to walk in the light and to thus expose sin as sin. Therefore, Paul says in Ephesians 5:14-17:

> ... Awake, you who sleep, arise from the dead, *and Christ will give you light.* See then that you walk circumspectly, not as fools but as wise, redeeming the time, because the days are evil. Therefore do not be unwise, but understand what *the will of the Lord is.*

Remember, God primarily responds to sin in one of two ways; forgiveness or judgment. Both grace and condemnation are expressions of light. Both are results of first exposing, confronting and convicting of sin. God's response depends on whether the individual repents or hardens his heart after he faces his own sin. Dealing with one's sin is, therefore, a requirement and prerequisite to encountering God.

Furthermore, the reality that sin must first be dealt with mandates the necessity for light. The absolute necessity for the sword of the Lord is thus created. It is absolutely essential to the foundation of the gospel that the Holy Spirit be allowed to convict of sin. We play a vital role in that effort, for we are to walk in light. That effort comes through our actions. The results will be based on how freely we allow the Spirit to flow through our actions and words.

Since we are to be like Christ, is there Biblical evidence that Jesus Himself incorporated the use of the sword when dealing with people? Look at this passage of scripture in Matthew 15:21-28:

> Then Jesus went out from there and departed to the region of Tyre and Sidon. And behold, a woman of

Canaan came from that region and cried out to Him, saying, "Have mercy on me, O Lord, Son of David! My daughter is severely demon-possessed." But He answered her not a word. And his disciples came and urged him, saying, "Send her away, for she cries out after us." But He answered and said, "I was not sent except to the lost sheep of the house of Israel." Then she came and worshiped him, saying, "Lord, help me!" But He answered and said, "It is not good to take the children's bread and throw it to the *little dogs*." And she said, "Yes, Lord, yet even the little dogs eat the crumbs which fall from their masters' table." Then Jesus answered and said to her, "O woman, great is your faith! Let it be to you as you desire." And her daughter was healed from that very hour.

One may ask what this has to do with confronting sin, but in reality that is exactly what Christ was doing. He confronted the woman right at the heart of the matter. She was calling on Him (verse 22). She was persistent (verse 23). She called Him Lord (verse 22). There is a strong indication, from her use of the term "son of David," that she recognized Him as the Messiah (verse 22). This seems to be verified in verse 25 when she "worshiped Him." So Jesus put her to the test to see if all that she was expressing was sincere. If she was motivated and dominated by sin, she would surely respond to His statement in a very predictable manner; likewise, if she had already confronted a large portion of her own sin, she would respond in an altogether different fashion. I think He was astonished at her response, given His expression, "O woman." The point is, He had brought a sword and He obviously was not afraid to use it. He shined an amazing amount of light on her, but she had already dealt with the area of darkness the Lord's blaze of light was aimed at detecting.

The rich young ruler in Luke 18:18-27 did not fare as well. The Lord shined some light into his heart and found there what He sought to detect. The sword of the Lord pierced deep within and revealed the man's hidden sin. For when Jesus observed this man's verbal and physical expressions, as he had those of the Syro-Phoenician woman, he said to the rich young ruler in verse 22, "... You still lack one thing. Sell all that you have and distribute to the poor, and you will have treasure in heaven; and come, follow Me." And the young ruler's response was this, according to Matthew 19:22, "But when the young man *heard that saying*, (author's note: the word or the sword of the Lord piercing him deeply) he went away sorrowful, for he had great possessions." Jesus was doing what light does, he was confronting darkness — He was confronting sin. The sword struck sin within the young ruler's heart.

Unless sin is dealt with in the way that God requires (a legitimate, divine confrontation of sin), there is no eternal value to whatever preaching, counseling or Bible studies in which we may participate. Sin must be dealt with, in order to come to a place of pleasing God.

In summary, we have seen this: the single greatest problem with the creation is sin. Sin will rob a person of eternal life; therefore, the sin of the individual must of eternal necessity be dealt with. For this reason, Jesus brought a sword to the earth as a part of His Messianic ministry. The Sword was Himself, the Word and the Light of God. This sword, (His Word and His Light) He used well on this earth, and passed it on to the Holy Spirit when He left, who now continues the ministry of the sword, desiring to use it through the Church, as required by God.

The wielding of the sword of the Lord is a ministry which confronts sin. It is not to be dispensed with meanness, guile or malice. It is not to be used as an excuse for exposing sin in another because someone has a chip on his shoulder or an anger problem, or is hiding a contentious spirit. It must be handled with godly motivation and intent.

The sword of the Lord is a ministry of confrontation aimed at exposing sin so that it can be properly dealt with by the blood and the cross of Christ. When properly used, it makes those who are perishing hateful. This is because they do not want their sin confronted, because they love darkness and hate the light.

Therefore, when the Church puts down the sword, the foremost ministry of Christ is stopped from being manifested upon the earth; at that point, the salt has lost its ability to season. The worst consequence of putting down the sword is that we, from God's perspective, move from a time of grace and mercy to a period of judgment.

When sin comes to the point where it is practiced openly without proper restraint — even tolerated due to a lack of confrontation — the wrath of God is kindled and He takes over the situation with national or cultural judgment. *God's judgment comes because of failure, not victory.* Judgment comes because the salt gave out or failed or became contaminated. His judgment comes because the Church has surrendered the sword of the Lord.

Chapter 6

It's a Matter of Authority – Jurisdiction – Sovereignty

Referring to God the Father in Matthew 6:10, Jesus taught us to pray specifically, "...Your will be done *on earth* as it is in heaven." This scripture reveals that the focus and concern of God is for His heavenly authority, influence and witness to be presented to the whole earth. As we have seen, this includes all areas. Nothing is left outside of His focus and concern. God's will is that the moral absolutes of His holy nature be observed by the creation which He made and sustains. It is God's desired goal, in fact, His nature demands, that His good should challenge and prevail over evil in all circumstances and situations. Therefore, He desires, and ultimately will require, that His moral principles be the foundation of all human social and cultural activity. It can be no other way; He is God. Furthermore, His moral absolutes are the values and standards by which all individuals are to govern and order their lives. For by His moral standard we will be judged.

God exists, and His very essence is moral perfection. These two truths mandate submission by the individual, as well as by "the kingdoms of men." In order to restore the proper role that God's moral values are to play in the day-to-day activities, norms and laws of a community, *God's people* must restore within themselves proper obedience to God's purpose, will and desires.

There is no doubt that the Holy Spirit is with us to restrain evil and to convict of sin. Why then is our culture deteriorating morally at such a fast rate?

The element needed (but lacking) in order to produce full restoration of His moral principles, is the manifestation of the properties of salt and light by His Church (the Body of Christ). For just as the Holy Spirit works through the foolishness of preaching (I Corinthians 1:21), He also works through the necessary ingredient of a public stand for righteousness. If there is no public passion or conviction manifested by those people in a community who say they belong to God, and there is no public declaration to the world of the absolute necessity that all things conform to God's divine nature, then there will be no great moving of the Holy Spirit. Conversely, wherever God's people truly adhere to His purposes, openly proclaiming God's Holy standards, a stage is being constructed upon which the Holy Spirit can work to restrain evil and convict of sin on a community-wide scale. Then the Holy Spirit's focus is upon the unsaved — not the saved. The end result of such a move is in His hands, but that partnership between the activity of the Church and the moving of the hand of God is critical, in order to bring it about.

God almost always chooses to work through human beings in order to influence the physical realm. Joseph, Daniel, Esther, Moses, Gideon and countless others attest to this fact. God has also chosen, in almost all cases, to respect the boundaries and requirements of the physical realm. For example, Jesus was required to take on human form and come into the physical realm in order to redeem the creation. Likewise the Church, working under and empowered by the Holy Spirit, is to be God's salt and light in the physical domain.

The Church is the vehicle by which God has chosen to press His claims over the creation and the creature.

The Church is not only the vessel selected to represent to this world the goodness of God as contained in the Gospel, but also the vessel chosen by God to proclaim the requirements of His holiness over every living soul, over every community of humankind, and over every social compact entered into by mankind.

Within the system of government which God has given us, each one of us carries a portion of the overall responsibility. Considering that we have a mission from God to be salt and light, and also that God Himself created government to promote good and punish evil, it is easy to see that every God-fearing person should, in every arena, actively represent the Spirit's concern that light overcome darkness and good overcome evil. I believe God would have His people represent His authority in every area of their community and national life, emphasizing the mandate for all to honor His jurisdiction over their lives and activities, both individually and as a nation.

Both one's acceptance of salvation and one's response to the Great Commission are based solely on a recognition of the authority and divinity of God: "But without faith it is impossible to please Him, for he who comes to God must believe that *He is...*" (Hebrews 11:6). *The most basic and vital piece of knowledge for man is that God is!* He is God and He is everything that the name implies. Do you perceive Him as He is? Is He God to you? Is He your God? (This is a question of sovereignty.) Does He have a right to call you into account? (This is a question of jurisdiction.) Have you submitted to Him as your God? (This is a question of authority.)

Jesus in Matthew 28:18-20 (the Great Commission), says:

> *All authority* has been given to Me in *Heaven and on earth.* Go *therefore* and make disciples of *all the nations,* baptizing them in the name of the Father and of the Son and of the Holy Spirit, *teaching them to observe all things that I have commanded you;* and lo, I am with you always, even to the end of *the age.*

Here we can apply the old adage that says: when you see a "therefore," you need to ask yourself what it is "there for." The underlying premise of the Great Commission is the matter of authority. Jesus said, "Go therefore..." The previously-stated reason for the disciples to go was that "all authority" had been given to Jesus, both in Heaven and on the earth.

By whose authority, according to Romans 13, do the nations govern themselves? It is God's authority, delegated to the nations by God Himself for the purpose of establishing good social order based upon God's perspective of good and evil. God's delegated authority for this arena, known as *civil authority,* has been placed under the lordship of Jesus. For all authority on the earth has been given to Jesus by God the Father. Based on that fact, Jesus said, "Go therefore, and make disciples of all the nations." The mandate is that His will is to be done by the whole earth — that all in Heaven and all on earth are gathered into One, even Jesus; therefore, the focus of the Great Commission is fixed on the nations. "Baptizing them..." is the presentation of salvation. "Teaching them to observe..." is the presentation of God's requirement that they live in accord with His righteousness. Let it be restated — this is so because salvation cannot be separated from the moral demands of God's holy nature. Obviously, only those who respond in a positive manner (the elect according to the foreknowledge of God) are going to be baptized and observe His requirements. However, the invitation — in fact, the need — to be baptized, like the teaching to observe, is presented to the nations, and they are required to observe the things Jesus commanded.

The Great Commission is about ultimate sovereignty because salvation is about ultimate sovereignty. Who is lord of your life, you or God? Are you, like Adam and Eve, also eating of the tree of the knowledge of good and evil, or have you, instead, given the fruit of that tree back to God? Only God can be morally perfect. Only God is capable of being right at all times, in all situations, within every circumstance. This was the very reason that the only activity forbidden to Adam and Eve in the garden, while they were living in harmony and fellowship with God, was the taking into and unto themselves of the decision-making power to determine what is good and what is evil.

For man to be morally perfect, he must allow God to be God of his life in all things. Getting from the condition we are in now to that state of being is a process which begins and is completed in Christ Jesus. That is God's plan. That process of restoration and regeneration begins at the point of salvation when we accept the Messiah, Jesus Christ of Nazareth, as both Lord and Saviour of our lives. Because we submit ourselves to God and His plan, and thereby relinquish power over our lives to His Christ, salvation is, indeed, a matter of sovereignty.

That is why the question of authority is foundational to the mission of the Great Commission. For someone to secure salvation, as it relates to his relationship with his Creator, he must deal with the reality of sin. Sin probably finds its most elementary definition, in Romans 3:23: "[F]or all have sinned and fall short of the glory of God...." At this level of understanding, any word, thought or deed that falls short of the standard that is God Himself, is sin in its most elementary form. God Himself is the only acceptable standard. That is why Jesus can say to us in Matthew 5:48: "Therefore you shall be perfect, just as your Father in heaven is perfect."

God's holiness — His moral perfection — is the standard. When we think about it, perfection is the only standard that makes sense. To accept anything short of that is to accept moral imperfection, and that is impossible for perfection to do. Morality cannot accept immorality as an equal because immorality is morally wrong. Purity allows only purity. It is the nature of purity to do so. It is as if you stood in an open space at noon on a sunny day; the light shining about you would not allow any darkness. It is the nature of physical light not to allow physical darkness. It is also the nature of moral light not to allow any moral darkness. God is perfection. God is purity. God is light. We all have fallen short of God's glory, which is His holiness, His moral purity and perfection. When an individual accepts the fact that he has sinned, he is acknowledging the reality that he is answerable to a higher moral authority than himself. That higher authority is the One True God.

Therefore, at the heart of the matter, salvation is a question of jurisdiction; it is a question of authority; it is a question of sovereignty. Those questions are settled properly when one seeks forgiveness from the Almighty for the infractions committed against His moral Nature. If the questions of jurisdiction, authority, and sovereignty are not settled properly with regard to God the Father, then how can we seek forgiveness from Him? For when we ask Him for forgiveness, we are acknowledging that He has jurisdiction over our lives. If we "believe that He is" God, then we will seek forgiveness from Him because that is the appropriate and correct response to God. If a person is not seeking forgiveness, neither is he seeking salvation nor, indeed, will he ever find it without submitting to God's authority, sovereignty and jurisdiction. That person will be eternally lost in his sin: Romans 3:23 in the New Living Translation says: "For all have sinned; all fall short of God's glorious standard."

If we are not seeking salvation, we are truly saying that we are taking authority and jurisdiction over our own lives. We are partaking of the fruit of the tree of the knowledge of good and evil. We are saying that we are capable of making morally perfect choices throughout the course of our lives. Or we are saying that we are not going to abide by what God says is right or wrong but that we will determine for ourselves what is right or wrong, ascribing or denying moral worth to some action or thought based upon our own desires. This mind-set denies God's rightful authority and thus rejects His sovereignty over our lives. If we reject submitting to God as God, we have also rejected godliness. For when we step off the path of moral perfection, we will be walking away from morality, no matter which way we go. For if we want moral perfection we must stay on God's path.

Satan tempted Eve with this statement in Genesis 3:5: "For God knows that in the day you eat of it your eyes will be opened, and you will be like God, knowing good and evil." Likewise, if we refuse to submit to God as God, by that very action we promote ourselves to the position of god unto ourselves. The problem with that action is that as a created being, we can never measure up to God's moral purity, which is at the core of all existence. We are dealing with the purity which belongs to absolute perfection. From the standpoint of eternity, this degree of divine light cannot permit any darkness. It is as impossible for moral light to allow darkness as it is for natural light to do so. The effect that light has on darkness, both natural and moral, is unavoidable and automatic.

Thus, we see that God will not, in fact cannot, ultimately allow sin to exist in that which He rules. Therefore, there will be a day of accountability, a moral audit that will determine who we have chosen to rule our lives, whether sin or God. The evidence that will be used to determine our choice will be our thoughts, words and deeds. At stake is where we will spend eternity. Those who choose God will accept Christ as their Savior and will escape this eternal judgment, but will still be held accountable. Holiness demands such an accounting. Moral light, which emanates from God's pure and holy nature, will not mix with darkness. It simply cannot happen.

For example, if for some reason it were necessary to preserve a quality known as absolute "dryness," then under no circumstances could it be mixed with any part of "wetness." Likewise, for all eternity, it is impossible for moral perfection to mix with immorality. They are forces that repel each other. Just like similar poles on two magnets, they simply cannot stay together. Likewise, physical light will dispel darkness; darkness can only exist were there is an absence of light. In the same manner, moral light and immoral darkness cannot mix — they repel — and light will forcibly remove darkness.

Paul writes concerning this light in I Timothy 6:11-16:

> But you, O man of God, flee these things and pursue righteousness, godliness, faith, love, patience, gentleness. Fight the good fight of faith, lay hold on eternal life, to which you were also called and have confessed the good confession in the presence of many witnesses. I urge you in the sight of God who gives life to all things, and before Christ Jesus who witnessed the good confession before Pontius Pilot, that you keep this commandment without spot, blameless until our Lord Jesus Christ's appearing, which He will manifest in His own time, He who is the blessed and only Potentate, the King of kings and Lord of lords, who alone has immortality, *dwelling in unapproachable light*, whom no man has seen or can see, to whom be honor and everlasting power. Amen.

Let's imagine, if we can, light so pure, virtue and righteousness so free of blemish that they have as a moral essence, an entirely transparent quality. Almighty God, having never done that which is wrong in all of eternity, is so hallowed, so morally pristine, that the possibility that He might do even the slightest wrong does not exist. His spiritual, moral perfection is so powerfully strong that the brilliance produced by it would consume the soul. The holiness of God is so sacred and pure that the splendor and majesty contained therein is nothing less than awesome. When the human creature is touched by even the *smallest* manifestation of His glory, it is so overwhelming that it will buckle the knees, make tears flood the eyes, and melt the heart under His mighty influence. This divine Person, the One True God, is the source and center of all existence — and His nature is holy. His holy nature radiates this moral light of which we speak.

On the coming Judgment Day, when every created being will stand before Him and His Christ, Almighty God will release a portion of this light. Literally every soul, including satan and the antichrist — under the sheer weight of the virtue and truth contained in that light — will voluntarily bow his knee and personally confess with his mouth that Jesus is both Christ and Lord.

Have you ever been in a situation in which, after you had done something wrong, the full realization of how wrong it was dawned on you? When this realization was combined with your fear of the possible consequences, did you become completely debilitated? Such an experience illustrates the reality of truth and justice in the daily activities of this life, when we face loved ones or temporal judgment. How then will we stand when we meet truth and justice in the person of God? How great will be the weight when we fully realize that our own condition for eternity is on the line? How debilitating will it be when we realize that the Judge we face knows every private action we've ever done, every single word we've ever uttered, every thought we've ever had. In fact, He knows every motive and intent of our hearts, and all of them will be used as evidence to prove whom we have chosen as *"god"* or God over our lives. Salvation is a matter of sovereignty.

That is why the opening scripture of this chapter is so relevant and important. Jesus prayed for God's will to be done on earth as it is in Heaven. And what is the fundamental issue as it pertains to God's will for the ages? We quoted it already in this book. Ephesians 1:10 said that God: "[M]ight gather in one all things in Christ, both which are in heaven and which are on earth — in Him." This primary purpose is known in scripture as "the mystery of His will" (Ephesians 1:9); and "the mystery of Christ" (Ephesians 3:4).

God's way of dealing with the problem of sin is to place everything into the life of His Son. Those found in Christ will be those who have accepted His sacrifice, which paid the price that moral perfection demands of immoral activity. His sacrifice *covers* now and forever and through the process of regeneration, *changes* the immoral darkness that is exposed in our lives by God's light. Colossians 1:7-29 says:

> [A]s you also learned from Epaphras, our dear fellow servant, who is a faithful minister of Christ on your behalf, who also declared to us your love in the Spirit. For this reason we also, since the day we heard it, do not cease to pray for you, and to ask that you may be filled with the knowledge of His will in all wisdom and spiritual understanding; that you may walk worthy of the Lord, fully pleasing Him, being fruitful in every good work and increasing in the knowledge of God; strengthened with all might, according to His glorious power, for all patience and longsuffering with joy; giving thanks to the Father who has qualified us to be partakers of the inheritance of the saints *in the light*. He has delivered us from the power of darkness and conveyed us *into the kingdom of the Son* of His love, in whom we have redemption through His blood, the forgiveness of sins. He is the image of the invisible God, the firstborn over all creation. For by Him all things were created that are in heaven and that are on earth, visible and invisible, whether thrones or dominions or principalities or powers. All things were created through Him and for Him. And He is before all things, and in Him all things consist. And He is the head of the body, the Church, who is the beginning, the firstborn from the dead, that in all things He may have the preeminence. For it pleased the Father that in Him all the fullness should dwell, and by Him to reconcile *all things* to Himself, by Him, whether things on earth or things in heaven, having made peace through

> the blood of His cross. And you, who once were alienated and enemies in your mind by wicked works, yet now He has reconciled in the body of His flesh through death, to present you holy, and blameless, and above reproach in His sight — if indeed you continue in the faith, grounded and steadfast, and are not moved away from the hope of the Gospel which you heard, which was preached to every creature under heaven, of which I, Paul, became a minister. I now rejoice in my sufferings for you, and fill up in my flesh what is lacking in the afflictions of Christ, for the sake of His body, which is the Church, of which I became a minister according to the stewardship from God which was given to me for you, to fulfill the word of God, *the mystery* which has been hidden from ages and from generations, but now has been revealed to His saints. To them God willed to make known what are the riches of the glory of this mystery among the Gentiles: *which is Christ in you*, the hope of glory. Him we preach, warning every man and teaching every man in all wisdom, *that we may present every man perfect in Christ Jesus*. To this end I also labor, striving according to His working which works in me mightily.

From God's perspective, "all things" in Heaven and earth were placed under the authority of Christ at the time of our Lord's resurrection and ascension. The Great Commission confirms this and from then until now, all authority dwells in His Christ. Confirming this Ephesians 1:17-23 says:

> [T]hat the God of our Lord Jesus Christ, the Father of glory, may give to you the spirit of wisdom and revelation in the knowledge of Him, the eyes of your understanding being enlightened; that you may know what is the hope of His calling, what

are the riches of the glory of His inheritance in the saints, and what is the exceeding greatness of His power toward us who believe, according to the working of His mighty power which He worked in Christ when He raised Him from the dead and *seated Him at His right hand in the heavenly places, far above* all principality and power and might and dominion, and every name that is named, *not only in this age*, but also in that which is to come. *And He put all things under his feet* and gave him to be head over all things to the church, which is His body, the fullness of Him who fills all in all.

When Christ Jesus took His place in heaven, seated next to His Father, it became evident to all who dwell in the spiritual realm that the transfer of authority was complete. All authority had at that point been placed in Christ's hands, including "all authority" here on earth. At that same point, God the Father began to subdue the enemies of His Christ — those who refuse to come under the authority of His Son. See again Hebrews 1:13, where God says to His Son, *"Sit at My right hand,* till I make Your enemies Your footstool."

Again, this all took place at the time of His ascension. For the Apostle Peter used the same scripture (Hebrews 1:13 and Psalms 110:1) in his preaching in Acts 2:34-35. In verses 32-33 he said, "This Jesus God has raised up, of which we are all witnesses. Therefore being exalted *to the right hand of God....*" And Stephen, just before he was stoned, proclaimed in Acts 7:56, "...Look! I see the heavens opened and the Son of Man standing at the right hand of God!"

At the time of His ascension into Heaven, Jesus was given by the decree of God the Father all authority in Heaven and on earth. The Great Commission is based upon this transfer of authority. It is important, even critical, that we understand the significance of the fact that all authority was transferred to Jesus at this specific time. Let us look again at the message delivered by the Apostle Peter in

Acts 2:36: "Therefore let all the house of Israel know assuredly *that God has* made this Jesus, whom you crucified, *both* Lord and Christ."

Scripture maintains the consistent theme that the wisdom and power behind the implementation of this plan is God Himself. God made Jesus the Messiah in order to bring salvation to the creation. He also made Him Lord, giving Him all authority over Heaven and earth. The Father is gathering all things into Jesus and He has placed all authority into our Lord's hands. This was accomplished at the point in time when Jesus died and rose from the dead. This truth is evidenced by the fact that after Jesus ascended, He assumed the position at the Father's right hand, according to the scriptures, and received from the Father the gift of the Holy Spirit which He gave to those who accept Him as Lord and Christ. God the Father then takes an active role in making Christ's enemies His footstool.

These, then, are the marching orders for the Church in this age: To bring everything into subjection to Christ, every philosophy and every high thing that exalts itself against the knowledge of God. Every thought is to be brought into obedience to Christ, for God has placed everything under His feet. This is God making the enemies of Christ His footstool.

It is important to see that a presentation of a gospel that does not clearly specify our Father's desire may not bring the respondent to a saving knowledge of Jesus Christ. A person who has an uneasy feeling or some kind of inner problem or reservation with the complete authority Jesus has over his life may have, at best, an area of his life not sanctified, or at worst, a soul that is not even saved. God has made Jesus Lord. If it is important to the Father that every living entity will ultimately bow the knee to His Son and confess that He is Lord, should not His people who have given their very lives to Him in salvation do so now? Especially considering that He is Lord of all. God Almighty, the One True God, has made Him so. If we fully understand salvation, we will know Him as such and call Him Lord.

Why then is not everything and everybody truly submitted to Christ? All things, by royal decree, have been put under the authority of Christ Jesus. God has made it so. Yet we do not see all things acting as though they were submitted to Christ. That is because this is the age of conflict in which light and darkness are contending for each and every soul. In that conflict, the Church is to press the claims of Christ over the life of the individual, and to publicly stand for righteousness, representing God's holiness and His moral jurisdiction over the creation. This complete and full witness is the precise stand that God desires for the Church. In my opinion, this is because that full and complete witness has the greatest chance of truly bringing the most souls to an actual saving knowledge of Christ Jesus our Lord. For it confronts the individual and the nation where they need to be confronted — and that is in the areas of sin, righteousness, and judgment.

This Christian confrontation is an essential element of authentic and orthodox Christianity because it is the method that God Himself uses. Hebrews 10:12-13 confirms this when it says, "But this Man, after He had offered one sacrifice for sins forever, sat down at the right hand of God, *from that time* waiting until His enemies <u>are made</u> His footstool." God is the one working to put these enemies under Christ at this present time, within this present age, and He desires to work through each one of us to bring every thought that is out there into obedience to Christ. This is an age of conflict, an age of confrontation. *The path to salvation is not paved with tolerance of sin, it is paved with forgiveness of sin.* Forgiveness requires repentance, and repentance requires conviction, and conviction requires moral light confronting moral darkness. The kingdom of this world is supposed to be confronted by the Kingdom of Heaven, that is, if God has a people on this earth who will be His salt and light.

God knows that the ultimate encounter with and the subsequent subjection of darkness will entail confrontation at its most extreme level. God will forcibly subdue the powers of darkness at the end of this age. We have seen earlier that Jesus will ride out of Heaven, leading an army, with the purpose of conquering the earth. For even though the authority over all the nations was given to Jesus at the time of his resurrection, this age has been a time period in which the nations, as well as individuals, have been given the opportunity for voluntary compliance.

Revelation 11:15 describes the scene in which the seventh angel blows the seventh trumpet: "...And there were loud voices in heaven, saying, *'The kingdoms of this world* have become the kingdoms of our Lord and of His Christ and He shall reign forever and ever!'" When Jesus and the armies of Heaven descend upon the earth, they will physically subdue the nations in order to force compliance with God's decree, will and plan. Then we see the final battle described in Revelation 19:17-21. Verse 19 says, "And I saw the beast, *the kings of the earth, and their armies*, gathered together to make war against Him who sat on the horse and against His army." And the results are recorded in verse 21, which says, "and the rest were killed with the sword which proceeded from the mouth of Him who sat on the horse...."

God is not the least bit afraid of confrontation or conflict, either now or in the future. In fact, in order to have the "new heavens and a new earth in which righteousness dwells," those committed to unrighteousness must be removed. God will remove them to the place that they have chosen. A place without God's influence, since that is what they desire. The choice is either for all of God or it is for none of Him, because God's moral perfection demands perfection and He will, therefore, ultimately have it.

In the interim, God, in His mercy, is giving each man every opportunity to make the right choice. Those who have chosen not to yield to God will gain that ultimate and total fulfillment of their choice: complete freedom from God. This situation is nonnegotiable — it is the ultimate confrontation. God is the only one who is capable of completing and willing to complete the necessary task, that which is required by the existence of moral perfection: the removal of that which has set itself against God. The choice will be final and irreversible, *even after man has fully realized the significance of an eternity without God's influence or involvement*. Revelation 19:20 says:

> Then the beast was captured, and with him the false prophet who worked signs in his presence, by which he deceived those who received the mark of the beast and those who worshiped his image. These two were *cast* alive into the lake of fire burning with brimstone.

Additionally, Revelation 20:11-15 says:

> Then I saw a great white throne and Him who sat on it, from whose face the earth and the heaven fled away. And there was found no place for them. And I saw the dead, small and great, standing before God, and books were opened. And another book was opened, which is the Book of Life. And the dead were judged according to their works, by the things which were written in the books. The sea gave up the dead who were in it, and Death and Hades delivered up the dead who were in them. And they were judged, each one according to his works. Then Death and Hades were cast into the lake of fire. This is the second death. And anyone not found written in the Book of Life was *cast* into the lake of fire.

The Greek word for "cast" is "ballo" which means to "throw or hurl." Using the evidence of their lives, God will establish that these individuals chose to separate themselves from the holy requirements of His nature; that they fail to live up to His standard of moral perfection; that they choose not to repent and accept His Son's sacrificial death as their covering and forgiveness from sin. Then, in order to have righteousness rule within a new creation, He will throw these individuals into the lake of fire that burns forever. Every person cast into the lake of fire will first be publicly convicted, based on the evidence, written in the books (the canvas of reality which is God), that this is actually the choice they made in refusing to submit to God. Therefore, God will give them over to an existence without Him.

Hebrews 6:1-2 says that the understanding of eternal judgment is one of the elementary principles of Christ. Why? Because it has to do with the most basic questions of eternity. Who is God? Is He actually God? Is He all that His name implies? Thus, is He morally holy and pure? And therefore, are we accountable to Him for our actions and thoughts?

That is why I say the fundamental question is one of sovereignty, jurisdiction and authority. Obviously, there is no question on God's part, "...He cannot deny Himself" (II Timothy 2:13). He knows who He is and He knows what must be done in order to free the creation from sin, as well as to bring as many people as possible into a right relationship with Him. We, His creation, must recognize that He is sovereign over all that exists, and that He has jurisdiction and authority over our very lives. He has the right to call for the return of our lives at any moment He so desires. For as we have seen, the very life that we are living is lived because of the pleasure, will and power of God. And He is sovereign over our very existence. Luke 12:16-20 says:

> Then He spoke a parable to them, saying: The ground of a certain rich man yielded plentifully. And he thought within himself, saying, "What shall I do, since I have no room to store my crops?" So he said, "I will do this: I will pull down my barns and build greater, and there I will store all my crops and my goods. And I will say to my soul, `Soul, you have many goods laid up for many years; take your ease; eat, drink, and be married.'" But God said to him, "Fool! This night *your soul will be required of you*; then whose will those things be which you have provided?"

This is a statement of absolute sovereignty revealing that God has authority and jurisdiction over every single soul as well as over all the governmental affairs of men (Remember Daniel 4:17: "...that the living may know that the Most High rules in the kingdom of men.") That is why the foundational premise to the Great Commission is that of God's authority and jurisdiction. The truth that God is exercising His right of divine sovereignty is at the heart of the Great Commission. At the inauguration of the Great Commission, God the Father, by divine order, placed all authority under the control of His Son, Jesus Christ of Nazareth. Remember, all authority is from God, including the authority by which governments function. The Father has placed all authority in Heaven and on earth into Christ's hands. That is why Isaiah 9:6 says, "...And the government will be upon His shoulder." Verse 7 adds, "Of the increase of His government and peace there will be no end...."

Therefore, the mandate of the Great Commission is pressing the claims of Christ over the life of the individual soul, stressing that God has moral jurisdiction and sovereignty over each man's very existence and over all that he is and does. In order to escape the automatic consequences of a choice that rejects the reality of Who He is, each man must accept and comply with the fact that there is a God who does and will rule.

Thus, the Great Commission compels us to make disciples of the nations because the nations operate by means of God's authority. *The nations are still directly under the authority of the King of Kings, whether or not they acknowledge Him, and they are required to function and operate just as God wants them to in this age of the sword.*

Chapter 7

The Wall

Since civil authority is actually ordained by God and thus required to reflect God's perspective of good and evil, the goal is to have a culture based on righteousness. God's people are to publicly proclaim and defend God's moral principles in an aggressive, confrontational posture, while at the same time reflecting humility and kindness. This public defense of God's principles has been lacking during the last several decades of this century. Because of that fact, the culture has progressed steadily downhill toward moral decay.

In order to please God and present to the world the witness that God requires, we must return to God's original plan. In order to restore our culture to a state in which God's righteousness is honored, we must once again be His salt and light. The only way to manifest the qualities symbolized by the terms "salt" and "light" is by submission to Christ so fully that our lives are not our own, but His. From that submission will come practical action that will convict of sin and restrain evil. *Is there time for Christians to act to bring restoration to our culture? With God, there is always time , and God lacks nothing in power, might or desire. He only waits for an obedient people.*

The scriptures teach principles of restoration that give us guidelines. After the Jews were led captive to Babylon they were eventually restored to the land that God promised them. First, a key principle in the restoration was obedient leadership. This need was met by three main individuals: Zerubbabel, Ezra and Nehemiah. There were three separate excursions back to Jerusalem, each led by one of these three leaders, beginning with Zerubbabel and ending with Nehemiah. Second, there were people who had given themselves to God's plan of restoration and were willing to follow these leaders.

Third, these people were committed to a complete restoration of their country, both spiritually and nationally. Fourth, their commitment was long-term. Taking into consideration the ups and downs that accompany even divine effort working through human beings (note that the prophet Malachi rebuked the returnees several times), the people stuck to their goal of achieving the restoration of what God had for them as His Covenant people.

After the people had embraced this vision, they established three *goals* for the restoration:

1) Rebuild the Temple
2) Restore public worship and obedience to the Law under the Old Covenant, and
3) Rebuild the wall of Jerusalem.

All three aspects of the restoration were, and are, important to God. The first two (from a New Testament perspective) relate to our relationship to God — our worship, our function in the Body of Christ and our public obedience to His Word and His moral nature. The third goal of restoration is political, for the building of the wall was an act of reestablishing Israel as a government — as a nation. Ezra 4:8-24 says:

> Rehum the commander and Shimshai the scribe wrote a letter against Jerusalem to King Artaxerxes in this fashion: From Rehum the commander, Shimshai the scribe, and the rest of the companions — representatives of the Dinaites, the Apharsathchites, the Tarpelites, the people of Persia and Erech and Babylon and Shushan, the Dehavites, the Elamites, and the rest of the nations whom the great and noble Osnapper took captive and settled in the cities of Samaria and the remainder beyond the River — and so forth. This is a copy of the letter that they sent him — To King Artaxerxes from your servants, the men of the region beyond the River, and so forth: Let it be known

to the king that the Jews who came up from you have come to us at Jerusalem, and are building the rebellious and evil city, and are finishing its walls and repairing the foundations. Let it now be known to the king that, if this city is built and the walls completed, they will not pay tax, tribute, or custom, and the king's treasury will be diminished. Now because we receive support from the palace, it was not proper for us to see the king's dishonor; therefore we have sent and informed the king, that search may be made in the book of the records of your fathers. And you will find in the book of the records and know that this city is a rebellious city, harmful to kings and provinces, and that they have incited sedition within the city in former times, for which cause this city was destroyed. *We inform the king that if this city is rebuilt and its walls are completed, the result will be that you will have no dominion beyond the River.* The king sent an answer: To Rehum the commander, to Shimshai the scribe, to the rest of their companions who dwell in Samaria, and to the remainder beyond the River: Peace, and so forth. The letter which you sent to us has been clearly read before me. And I gave the command, and a search has been made, and it was found that this city in former times has revolted against kings, and rebellion and sedition have been fostered in it. There have also been mighty kings over Jerusalem, who have ruled over all the region beyond the River; and tax, tribute, and custom were paid to them. Now give the command to make these men cease, that this city may not be built until the command is given by me. Take heed now that you do not fail to do this. Why should damage increase to the hurt of the kings? Now when the copy of King Artaxerxes' letter was read before Rehum, Shimshai the scribe, and their companions, they went up in haste to Jerusalem against the Jews, and by force of arms made them cease. Thus the work of the house of God which is at Jerusalem ceased, and it was discontinued until the second year of the reign of Darius king of Persia.

The concern over the Jews was not that some had returned to Jerusalem, nor, to any great extent, that they had rebuilt the Temple (though some didn't even want that to happen). The intense concern was openly expressed when they intended to rebuild the wall.
The dynamic here is that the people of the world do not care what people do privately. They say, "Go ahead and build your temples." **But if and when what God's people do in the temple becomes significant and spills out and begins to affect government and public opinion, that is an entirely different matter.**
And that is what the concern was here. When the people of Israel reestablished themselves openly, it threatened the authority of others.

In like manner, the devil may not be concerned with what goes on in our Churches for long periods of time. However, when we become obedient to God and begin to press the claims of Christ and God's righteousness, all hell will literally break loose as light challenges darkness. When we proclaim Christ's authority, all other authority is challenged.

In this age of the New Covenant, the *wall to reconstruct*, for the purpose of bringing civil government back to its proper place (that of reflecting God's perspective of good and evil), is our public stand in the civil arena of our day (*"before men ... for righteousness' sake..."*). This public stand will also establish a national identity that honors and submits to God's moral absolutes. God's people will always engage in an open public expression of righteousness when they are in obedience to His will and nature. As the wall at Jerusalem had to be rebuilt in order for Israel to reemerge as a government (nation), the *wall* of letting our light shine before men, so that morality may influence government, must be restored today. The public expression of standing *for* righteousness and *against* unrighteousness has been woefully absent from the witness of the

Church over the last several decades.

Because the people of Israel neglected God's will and holiness, they were judged and fell into the hands of their enemies. They completely lost their right to an open corporate expression of who they were as God's people. Did you hear that? Through disobedience, they lost their right before God to express themselves corporately as His people. Remember this was a full and complete expression or witness. It incorporated the entire will of God ranging from the religious to the civil, and including everything in between. But in their loss, God subjected them in hope because the promises He made to Abraham, David, etc., are covenant promises. Those who understood the eternal designs and purposes of God as His plan unfolded throughout the ages knew that restoration had to come in order for these promises to be fulfilled. In His timing, God started the restoration process in order to restore *His people* to His purpose and plan. In order to restore them to a place that was in line with God's purposes, the temple had to be rebuilt. Public religious observance needed to be reinstated and the wall restored.

Similarly, if we are going to be pleasing to God, the Church (His temple on earth) needs to be constructed as the Body of Christ. We must also *"teach them to observe all things that I have commanded you,"* a mission which corresponds to the rebuilding of the public religious observances of the people. And we must rebuild the wall — civil authority obedient to God, and a national wall of moral principle that brings about public policy which reflects God's understanding of good and evil.

After Zerubbabel had returned to build the Temple, and after Ezra had worked to restore the spiritual and moral condition of those who returned, Nehemiah led the third remnant who were returning with the burden to finally rebuild the wall. Although it was also on the heart of the first two leaders to build the wall, in God's providence, it fell to Nehemiah to complete the vision. Much more can be said about the restoration as well as about Zerubbabel and Ezra, but for our discussion, the important points to draw from the book of Nehemiah are these:

    1) There was a clear desire to restore;

2) There was willingness to turn that desire into physical action;
3) There was a commitment to follow the leadership;
4) There was resolution to face and to stand up to criticism, name calling and physical threats;
5) There was the aim to be obedient to God's purposes;
6) There was an acceptance of responsibility by each person for the restoration of a geographical section of work;
7) There was a spirit of cooperation among the participants as they worked together;
8) There was supernatural work by God on their behalf because of their obedience as expressed in points 1-7.

The construction of the wall meant the reemergence of the commonwealth of Israel. It was a statement "before men," signifying the national or governmental expression of the purposes and will of God working within His people. God works His complete will within all the different areas of life and within each person who is completely yielded to Him. God desires that His people are completely balanced in "rightly dividing the word of truth." His people are not allowed to pit the importance of one requirement against the importance of another in order to avoid the responsibility of the one that, for what ever reason, they do not want to perform. We are not allowed to say that prayer is so important that its fulfillment alleviates our obligation to God to be good fathers, mothers, husbands or wives, nor does the obvious importance in saving souls alleviate our obligation to be involved with God in the political process of our communities and nation. In fact, *this involvement — standing publicly for righteousness (being salt and light to this world) — is a vital ingredient to the evangelistic process that God desires. This is what must be restored. This is the wall that needs to be rebuilt. This wall, by its very nature, is the public adherence to God's righteousness that will impact the government, politics and our na-*

tional identity.

Nehemiah and those who returned with him responded in obedience to God, accepting His will to restore what He wanted to restore in the physical realm. This action upset those who, for a variety reasons, did not want an open witness of God's righteousness or His purposes for the creation.

The same is true today, just as it has been and will be throughout history. As long as unrighteousness is unrestricted within the creation, it will thrive in its prime motivation and activity, which is to gain supremacy over God's moral principle, publicly as well as within the soul of the individual. The present effort to keep all moral religious expression out of the public arena is merely a continuation of that unrighteous crusade. For when all is said and done, this remains the ongoing struggle between God and satan. And there is no neutral ground. If God's people are "absent without leave" (AWOL), it works for the direct benefit of the enemy.

During the time period of Nehemiah there would have been no restoration if there had not been individuals who were willing to be obedient to God's call and purposes. Remember, not all of the Jews came back from captivity. Many remained in Babylon. But *enough* of the people returned with a yearning to do God's purposes. Therefore, God was able to use them to restore in the physical realm what He desired for all to see; a visible *expression* of His temple; a visible *expression* of public devotion to Him and a visible *expression* of their national identity, the governmental and political concerns of God.

It was the restoring of Israel's national identity that upset the governmental authorities surrounding Jerusalem. Though they did not want any of the three *goals* (e.g., *expressions*) of restoration, the "wall" represented a higher level of permanence, order and activity (i.e. civil law, military, trade, etc.) to the other *expressions* because it was on a governmental or national level.

Likewise, the enemies of God today insist that the things of God have to be taken from government and politics. Nothing is further from the truth, for God, who created civil government, is politically involved. But as it is today, so it was then; the enemies of God did not want the wall built. But back then, as Nehemiah 4:6

says, "So *we built the wall*, and the entire wall was joined together up to half its height, *for the people had a mind to work.*" So it would be today, if there were a restoration of obedience and commitment by God's people to the full purpose and will of God.

Nehemiah knew that the construction of the wall brought protection for every other *expression*. **By contrast, today, because the bulk of God's people have ignored the government, "the wall" that should be there to protect, is not. Hence, it is from the government (through the broken wall) that the attacks are coming against the things of God.**

I contend that because God created government and the nations, (see Acts 17:26), He is personally involved in the politics of those nations. Both reason and scripture assert that those in whom He resides will manifest that same desire for involvement and concern for government. Just as those Jews with Nehemiah were burdened to rebuild the wall and reestablish their government and nation, we also should feel that same burden within us, because there was a "time you were without Christ, being aliens *from the Commonwealth of Israel* and strangers from the covenants of promise, having no hope and without God in the world" (Ephesians 2:12). However, because we are now *in Christ* we are "Now, therefore ... no longer strangers and foreigners, *but fellow citizens* with the saints and members of the household of God" (verse 19). Both of these terms, *commonwealth* and *citizens*, are governmental in nature because God, in addition to being many wonderful things, is also governmental in Nature. The substance of all that He is, His will, His Nature, His purposes, His Spirit resides in our hearts, flows through our spirits and works within our souls. And He is the same God Who created government itself; the same God Who created all the nations; the same God Who made a nation for Abraham and established the commonwealth of Israel; the same God Who worked within the varied governments of Egypt, Assyria, Babylon, Persia and countless others; the same God Who made us fellow citizens with the saints in the commonwealth of Israel. That same God is in our hearts. For Romans 11:17-18 says:

> And if some of the branches were broken off, and

you, being a wild olive tree, were grafted in among them, and with them, became a partaker of the root and fatness of the olive tree, do not boast against the branches. But if you do boast, remember that you do not support the root, but the root supports you.

Two things are undisputable in these scriptures. The first is that it is God who flows through the root and through the tree to the branches. Verse 23 says, "God is able." He is the divine life who will cause all His plans to be fulfilled. The second is that we have been grafted into the same ongoing reality of purpose which motivated Zerubbabel, Ezra and Nehemiah in restoring God's will and intent within this physical realm. The same reality of purpose was present with Joseph in Egypt, Esther in Persia, Daniel in Babylon, John the Baptist in Jerusalem (who confronted Roman power), and with our Founding Fathers in pre-revolutionary America, the men who confronted King George III of England.

The same reality of purpose exists in God at this present time. God's involvement in government and His desire for a nation of people was part of His promise to Abraham, was His reason for sending Joseph to Egypt, and was part of the purpose for sending Nehemiah and the others back to Jerusalem. He was present with our Founding Fathers at the birth of the United States of America. It was in the heart of God to create government and it is in His heart to be involved in governments. God has a desire in His heart for government to reflect His goodness. He has a desire toward the nations to disciple them in the ways of Christ. Within God's heart there remains a desire to have a nation of people devoted to Him. Therefore, it should be no surprise that our Founding Fathers, believing in God and receiving motivation and encouragement from Him, built their nation accordingly. Nor, considering God's concern with these matters, is it a surprise that Nehemiah found himself in Jerusalem, committed to rebuilding the wall of the city. Nor was it contrary to Daniel's knowledge of God and His ways for him to work toward good government, even within a pagan culture like that of Babylon, because God is politically involved.

God was involved with Nehemiah and the remnant in reestablishing the nation of Israel after years of captivity. And that remnant, the people who came out of captivity, had a mind to work. That is the way nations are built and that is the way nations are restored. Under Nehemiah's leadership, the people became as one man in order to accomplish the task. The construction of the wall commanded by God became their number-one priority. Nehemiah's confidence in the rebuilding of the wall and his answer to the critics is found in Nehemiah 2:20: "So I answered them, and said to them 'The God of heaven *Himself* will prosper us; therefore we *His servants* will arise and build....'"

And build they did. Chapter 3 is entitled by the translators, the "Record of the Builders." This chapter describes a unique concept in the restoration process, in which the builders divided themselves into groups, and each group took a certain section of the wall to build. Thirty-two verses describe different sections of the wall that were being restored by various groups and individuals. Such a pattern that would work today, because it has obviously been proved. If everyone were to make the type of commitment that the builders of the restoration did, I believe that, under God's direction, we would see the same successful results. The Jews built a physical wall, reestablishing their national identity under God. We build a spiritual wall of moral principle which also reestablishes a national identity, one that is also based on God's will and covenant. And as with the Jews, it will take physical effort on our part.

As the wall of Jerusalem needed workers for its rebuilding, so also does our wall today. Ours lies in the same shambles as did theirs before they restored it. The only difference between our circumstances and theirs is their deeper understanding of what God wanted of them and their greater willingness to work. As each of them worked on a section of the wall, so each one of us should be responsible for an area of the restoration of moral principle in our civil life.

Under God, our American Founding Fathers built a wall, that is, a nation with a very distinct national and moral identity. Under God, we have been required to maintain the wall they built. If we, through our neglect, have allowed the wall to be destroyed then we, under God, become responsible for the restoration of that wall. At this very moment in history, we are standing at that point of responsibility. The political, moral wall of our society lies in ruins, and the only way to restore it is to rebuild it. That takes work. The people were extremely focused in Nehemiah's day, as were our Founding Fathers in theirs. Chapter six, verses fifteen and sixteen says:

> So the wall was finished on the twenty-fifth day of Elul, *in fifty-two days*. And it happened, when all our enemies heard of it, and all the nations around us saw these things, that they were very disheartened in their own eyes; for they perceived that *this work was done by our God.*

The nation of Israel was back — the commonwealth of Israel was restored. God was with them because they had committed themselves to His purposes. Likewise today, if we submit to God's will and purposes, He will be with us in the restoration process.

Those who would like to be listed in the Record of the Builders may ask, "Where then is my section of the wall?" You need only step out onto your front porch and look around — behold your section of the wall. Your section of the wall, at the minimum, could be your family, friends, and acquaintances. Or, if you yield to His will in a greater way, the burden that God gives you could make your neighborhood, town or city your section of the wall — maybe even your state or nation.

Remember that the goals of restoration are threefold:

1) Rebuild the temple (restoration of the fully-functioning Body of Christ, in all aspects);
2) Restore the spiritual, moral and social well-being of the citizens; and
3) Reconstruct the wall — the national identity.

The specific burden that the Lord gives may focus a person more passionately in one of these directions, but that will never take from him the responsibility of laboring to carry out God's complete will and purpose for all areas of restoration. At the very least, we are meant to fulfill our responsibility to God to stand for righteousness within our sphere of influence.

Many will be called, as were Nehemiah, Joseph, and John the Baptist, to serve in a greater or more specific capacity, but all are called to be involved. This is God's will. According to His will, the world is to see the people of God demonstrating a courageous, yet compassionate witness of His divine purposes and nature. The scope of that witness must, of necessity, include government, the arena through which God desires to manifest His light and righteousness to bring His desired order to the "affairs of men."

Therefore, it is incumbent upon God's people, His visible representatives on the earth, to ensure that government functions as God desires. This is part of the manifestation of salt and light. In fact, being salt and light will impact all of the society and culture that we are part of. If every person were obedient, then every nation would reflect the goodness of God in the workings of government and political life. If we are yielding completely to God, out of our hearts will flow a concern that His will and goodness be seen in and through all the areas of human activity. Through the motivation and desire instilled in them by God, His people are required to put forth the effort to bring "every thought into captivity to the obedience of Christ," no matter where in the culture such a thought "exalts itself against the knowledge of God..."

Since God has an interest in government, so will we — if we allow Him to influence our lives completely.

Chapter 8

Matters of a Practical Nature

Since we live in a constitutional republic (at least that was the intent of our Founding Fathers), the direction of our government is our responsibility. This is true because "we the people" retain the democratic right of electing our representatives. Without question, therefore, the quality of our elected representatives directly determines the quality of our government, which is also then an accurate reflection of who we are as citizens and voters. Consequently, the standards and values we use when determining our vote makes the person elected a direct representation of the collective standards and values of the majority. It can be no other way.

You may say, "Most of the time, I just hold my nose and vote," but you must realize that this method of voting sets negative standards and values. Voting is an action which has consequences; therefore, voting is either a moral act or an immoral act — depending upon the events set in motion, the results accomplished by the vote cast. Our vote is an expression of one consideration having greater importance than another. Therefore, the way we vote expresses those considerations which have ultimate value to us. "For where your treasure is, there your heart will be also" (Matthew 6:21). What you deem to be most important will determine how you will ultimately vote — even if you hold your nose. Holding your nose could simply mean that the vote you are casting truly stinks.

When we vote, we are stating the level of good that we demand in government, or else we are indicating how unimportant, in our judgment, moral principle really is. Voting is an expression of how much evil we will tolerate or not tolerate. It is an inescapable reality that what the majority tolerates today becomes the standard tomorrow, especially in elections.

This was clearly demonstrated in November of 1996 in Oregon when a Republican was elected to the U.S. Senate, and then gave his open support to the Employment Nondiscrimination Act (ENDA), which grants minority status based on homosexuality. Electing this man with his acceptance of open sin in defiance of God, established a new Republican standard for supposed non-liberals. We could see that standard at work in the 1997 Oregon legislative session, after his campaign and election, when a record twelve *unRepublicans* voted to support a state version of ENDA. That senator's support of rights based on homosexuality was used as an argument on the House floor; his open public stand in support of that part of the homosexual political agenda gave political cover for the twelve *unRepublicans*. They undoubtedly felt confident that if the voters would not hold an elected official accountable for supporting ungodliness, then neither would they be held accountable by the voters when they support immorality. That is what happens when we hold our noses and vote for someone we shouldn't. Our vote actually assists in the advancement of evil.

Thus, the way we vote can create a standard that works against God's holiness. The opposite is equally true. We can recreate moral standards within our culture only by placing the same importance which God does upon the moral principles that He advocates. Therefore, the only way to reestablish moral standards is to openly express the standard that needs to be reinstituted — and then hold to it no matter what, never wavering, never compromising. For if we compromise a moral standard which, with our mouths, we say is important, our action is saying that the inducement compelling us to compromise is really more important. Otherwise we would not have chosen the compromise over the moral principle. The action of compromise loudly says that whatever prompted us to compromise is of greater import than the moral principle. For if the moral standard had been more important to us, we would have chosen to remain loyal to it. If our vote compromises our standard, we have nullified our testimony that proclaims the moral superiority of the standard. Our action establishes the superiority of whatever compelled us to compromise.

Within that framework though, there is always room to accept part of what we are after, as long as we do not compromise our public commitment to the restoration of the full standard of morality to which God holds us. We should publicly proclaim the moral standard, and then work to win converts to it until a new majority can be rebuilt around the standard. But to our shame, in our voting and in numerous other ways, we have compromised God's moral absolutes over and over again. We have progressively elected weaker candidates, election cycle after election cycle. Because we have compromised in our voting for candidates, our elected representatives, once they are in office, feel perfectly free themselves to compromise on moral principle when voting on legislation. That is the reason that for over three decades our culture has been spiraling downward from one essentially based upon moral principle to one that is based upon principles of decadence and licentiousness. We have tolerated moral decay and, therefore, increased moral decay is what we have received.

Ever-increasing public immorality is the *offspring* of the toleration of open sin. When we grow accustomed to open sin and when we tolerate actions that defy God's moral requirements, then because of the dullness, coldness and cowardice of our own hearts, we will elect people who will establish public policy which reflects that same hardened attitude and tolerance of evil. Since this is exactly what has been occurring, the only way to change it is to break the cycle that created it. Therefore, we must establish the policy that we will not compromise God's moral absolutes, either privately or publicly, through our voting or in any other way.

We are on this earth to publicly support God's moral principles. No other notion or consideration is more important. God does not condone subordinating such moral issues as the value that He places on human life to the mere exercise of electing Republicans over Democrats or Democrats over Republicans. He requires us to walk (which means all human activity, including voting) in the light and in the Spirit. I can say with confidence, before God, that anyone who casts even a single vote for someone who will support abortion, homosexuality, pornography, suicide or the like is not being motivated to do so by His divine light or Holy Spirit. His light or

His Spirit will never prompt anyone to support or associate with wrongdoing. The Scripture says in I Timothy 5:22, "Do not lay hands on anyone hastily, nor share in other people's sins; keep yourself pure." This principle applies, in varying degrees, to all aspects of life. For example, in business an employer does not hire someone without the qualifications, work history and references to meet his requirements. Nor does anyone get a promotion without having been proved. A good businessman would never trust his company with someone who did not meet his standards. He would neither fill a position nor give a promotion until a person fulfilled his requirements. This is consistent with the principle of the passage from I Timothy. But for some reason, we do not allow this logic to follow through in politics. For most people, the fact that a candidate is registered Republican or Democrat, depending on one's mind-set, is sufficient reason to vote for him. Yet, it is my contention that the principle of holding to a high standard should apply throughout life — from the Church — to the military — to the hiring of a babysitter — to voting.

One may say, "Politics is different, it's a winner-take-all situation." Yes, it is a winner-take-all situation, but there is no difference. Godly principles are eternal and absolute, and when we violate them, the end result will be the opposite of godliness. Ungodliness is what we now have, manifesting itself at every level throughout the political arena, the government and the culture. Why? Because you and I have violated God's principles and holiness by casting our votes for people who then use their authority and position to advance policy and law contrary to God's principles and holiness. If this is not so, then our nation should have no worries about the approach of divine judgment. And we should have no apprehension about explaining before God the reason our culture (in which we are supposed to be God's salt and light) finds itself in the position of awaiting pending judgment.

We must acknowledge that *the many* (the majority) have actually voted into public office the very people who have implemented the laws which have promoted the abominations that are now ushering in divine judgment. It seems that most people make their decisions without regard for God's moral requirements and His will.

But God is not mocked. When His moral requirements are violated and sin is tolerated openly and even passed into law, there begins a slow, steady advance toward the time when God's wrath will be poured out because of, and upon, the very things that *the many* are tolerating. The question is — are we part of *the many*?

Remember our opening premise: *We are privileged to participate in a democratic constitutional republic*, a form of government in which we elect the people who make the laws and set the policy standards. If I vote for someone who ultimately helps pass a law or set a policy contrary to God's moral nature, am I a partaker of the sin committed by that legislator — or is the act of voting outside the realm of God's sovereignty? If it is, why is He then going to divinely judge (an act which is an expression of His Sovereignty) the nation or culture whose laws and standards violate His moral nature? Considering that God will pour out His wrath on a culture, nation or community (which He has done and will do again, because of conduct that is proscribed by His holiness), it would seem that He takes more than just a cursory interest in what goes on in the arena of politics and government. And since He will condemn temporal nations and cultures, how will He look upon those people who have assented to and assisted in the establishment of condemnable things in the culture which He is now going to judge?

If we hold our noses and vote for someone who will advance sin, the holding of our noses does not nullify or diminish the fact that we actually voted to advance sin. When God's wrath begins to build toward divine judgment, we will not escape His displeasure if we have participated in creating the very situation which prompted His wrath.

If we walk in the light — let us also vote in the light. If we do not vote "in the Spirit" we are saying that God is not sovereign over that activity. Yet we have already seen that all authority, even civil authority, is from God and that the Holy Spirit calls elected officials His "ministers" who serve in the civil arena.

Some would even acknowledge that God rules over this arena — that He even created it to accomplish His intended purpose, and that He considers those who serve in the arena of civil authority to be ministers of His, expecting them to reflect His understanding of good and evil. Yet knowing all of this, they still condone and facilitate the politics of electing God's "ministers" by means of the flesh, i.e., by betraying friends to gain political power, lying and compromising beliefs to gain access, advancement and financial support. The spectacle of Christians walking in deception, thinking that God will sanction the use of worldly attitudes and conniving to determine who is to represent His moral goodness in the civil arena, must cause the devil to rub his hands together with glee. Much has been accomplished by satan in the tearing down of public adherence to God's moral standards. The sad thing is that in many cases he has used Christians to help him. The thought that many of God's people have been assisting God's enemy is staggering and shameful. However, if all of His people had made a commitment not to compromise on issues which involve God's moral absolutes, we would not now have acceptance and even open promotion of such abominations as abortion, pornography, and homosexuality. To be even an indirect participant in such offenses is to walk according to the ways of this world — it is to act in darkness. To put worldly considerations above the divine will is exactly what many Christians have been doing, and yet the scripture says in Romans 12:2, "And do not be conformed to this world, but be transformed by the renewing of your mind, that you may prove what is that good and acceptable and perfect will of God." And I Corinthians 6:19-20 says:

> Or do you not know that your body is the temple of the Holy Spirit who is in you, whom you have from God, and you are not your own? For you were bought at a price; therefore glorify God in your Body (author's note: except when your body votes?) and in your spirit, *which are God's*.

God owns your body and your spirit at all times except, of course, when you vote. Everybody knows that when you cast your vote, your body and spirit belong to the Republican Party or the Democrat Party, as the case may be. That is how most Christians act. From the standpoint of the Kingdom of God, that's utter nonsense! Jesus did not shed His blood for us, purchasing us out of sin and eternal damnation, in order for us to vote in a manner that elects individuals who will work against Him, using God's own delegated authority to do so. If we are obedient to His principles and His Spirit, God will raise up leaders who we *can* support. If we have accepted Jesus as our Lord and Savior, then we are not our own and all our thoughts and actions, including voting, belong to Him. James 3:10-18 says:

> Out of the same mouth proceed blessing and cursing. My brethren, these things ought not to be so. Does a spring send forth fresh water and bitter from the same opening? Can a fig tree, my brethren, bear olives, or a grapevine bear figs? Thus no spring yields both salt water and fresh. Who is wise and understanding among you? Let him show by good conduct that his works are done in the meekness of wisdom. But if you have bitter envy and self-seeking in your hearts, do not boast and lie against the truth. This wisdom does not descend from above, but is earthly, sensual, demonic. For where envy and self-seeking exist, confusion and every evil thing are there. But the wisdom that is from above is first pure, then peaceable, gentle, willing to yield, full of mercy and good fruits, without partiality and without hypocrisy. Now the fruit of righteousness is sown in peace by those who make peace.

Though this passage of scripture is referring specifically to the problem of uttering both "blessing *and* cursing" with the same tongue, the examples of which the Apostle says, "these things ought not to be so," represent universal principles. Two entirely opposite products cannot come forth from the same source, the purpose of which is to produce only one type of product. Thus, a fig tree cannot produce olives, nor can a fountain or spring flow simultaneously with bitter water and sweet. When this Biblical principle is applied to I Corinthians 12, the question arises: Can people who have agreed to be bought with the blood of Jesus Christ and are, therefore, no longer their own, feel free to act as if they are their own? Many of God's people are doing just that when it comes to voting. In casting their ballots, they ignore the moral attributes and absolutes of God, Who motivated and developed the plan that sent His Son to the earth to pour out His blood as the price of their salvation. The many have been subordinating moral principles and other considerations, and electing individuals who then use their positions to establish public policy that is contrary to God's holy nature, thus undermining God's morality in the culture.

So the fact is, *the many* are voting against God. No wonder the society is in such bad shape. With so many of God's people voting in a manner that aids and abets satan, we are reaping the only results possible — a culture in a process of decay, clearly visible to all. Our present situation exists because you and I have not done our duty as God's people. So many of us have ignored His concerns and focused on worldly interests. This has created a void in which there is no Godly restraint to the increase of evil (not to be confused with the Holy Spirit's restraint of the son of perdition in II Thessalonians 2:6-7). The fault and responsibility for this situation rests squarely with you and me because the Holy Spirit wants to restrain and even overcome the darkness through us. For we are God's salt and light. If we don't manifest those qualities, no one else will. The increase of evil obviously reveals that we are not fully yielding to the Holy Spirit.

Many hold to what they call a *gradualist* philosophy, as opposed to what they dub a *purist* position. Using football terminology, some have said it's like the difference between going for a five-yard gain and a first down, compared to throwing a long bomb for a touchdown. The use of the word *gradualist* and of the football metaphor may be convenient and appealing. It is, however, misleading and inaccurate because it obscures the real issue and the reason for rightful opposition to *gradualism*. It is an assertion that God's people can compromise His moral absolutes as they support, work with and vote for individuals who are running for public office.

The scriptures cited in this book teach us that we cannot support anything which advances evil — absolutely never. However, we can support anything that takes back positive moral ground even though it may not, at that time, gain the restoration of an entire moral principle in our culture. That is true only if our public stand, observable in both word and deed, supports the restoration of the moral principle in its entirety. On the abortion issue, for example, we may try to stop second and third trimester abortions through legislation or the initiative process, because we know most people will vote to save some of the babies. At the same time, we must take the public stand that all life is precious in God's eyes, and then continue to work for the elimination of all abortion and work toward positive alternatives, such as adoption, and the supporting of crisis pregnancy centers.

No individual who believes in the One True God, the God of Abraham, Isaac and Jacob, the Father of our Lord Jesus Christ should ever cast a single vote for a candidate whose personal philosophy and energy, manifested through word or deed, works to establish public policy that advances or promotes sin. Dr. Dobson was right when he said at a pro-life rally in Washington, D.C., *"I have determined that for the rest of my life, however long God allows me to live on this earth, I will never cast one vote for any man or woman who would kill one innocent unborn baby."* The day he made that pledge, I agreed and took the Dobson pledge myself. God does not allow us to subordinate the value He puts on life to mere political considerations, nor does He allow us to subordinate any other moral dictate of His holiness.

Civil government, in this age, is supposed to uphold the basic concept of moral good and be a terror to immorality and evil. In our constitutional republic, we are supposed to elect people who will do just that. Those for whom we vote are to be *"God's ministers"* (Romans 13:4), not candidates whose personal philosophy would promote legislation and public policy contrary to God's divine nature, purposes and will. We are not to elect individuals who will use God's delegated authority to praise evil and terrorize good. Would God prompt you to do such a thing, contradicting His own pattern and word? Of course not! Therefore, if anyone advocates that you do so, it is against the will of God. A wisdom that encourages God's people to support those who advance concepts and practices that are in open opposition to God's moral nature does not come from above. As we saw in an earlier chapter, God does not tempt people to do wrong.

In the 1990 governor's race in Oregon many gradualists advocated supporting a Republican who was one hundred percent against God's moral positions on all the social issues, such as abortion and homosexuality. So much so, that he marched in a pro-abortion demonstration and allowed his name to be used as one of its sponsors. He also attended a National Abortion Rights Action League (NARAL) fund-raising banquet, the proceeds of which were designated to defeat pro-life candidates in Oregon. Added to his disqualifying moral stands, this Republican wasn't even a fiscal conservative. Some would have classified him as a socialist; he may have been a liberal at best. At that time the gradualist philosophy was used to advocate Christian support for this individual.

The old saying goes, "actions speak louder than words." This adage could aptly apply to *gradualism*. Behind its curtain of partial logic, it gives the freedom to politically support individuals whose philosophy advocates varying degrees of immorality. This might be acceptable if politics and government were separate from God's sovereignty and holy nature. But as we've seen, they are not; therefore, at the very least, a basic commitment to righteousness must be sought, followed and maintained in the political and governmental spheres. For the simple fact remains; if the salt takes on the characteristics of the world, who will challenge and restrain worldliness?

Gradualists use Exodus 23:30 as their Biblical basis; it reads, "Little by little I will drive them out from before you, until you have increased, and you inherit the land." However following that, verse 31 says: "And I will set your bounds from the Red Sea of the Philistines, and from the desert to the River. For I will deliver the inhabitants of the land into your hand, and I will drive them out before you."

I agree, obviously, with the premise of verse 30 and do not take exception with the principle of progressing step by step, battle by battle. But in verses 30 and 31, the main gist is that God will *drive them out*; the rate at which He will do it is secondary. Something must be happening before it can be determined how fast it will happen. What God is doing in verses 30 & 31 is *"driving them out."* It doesn't sound as if He wants us to vote for them, does it? If we're going to use verse 30 to support *gradualism*, then let's act within the whole context and vote to *drive them out* of office.

Let me ask some questions: When the Jews, to whom the word in verse 30 was spoken, came out of the wilderness after the forty-year exile and encountered Jericho (which was also their first battle), were they required to be totally obedient to God? Yes, completely! Were they allowed to make a coalition or a deal with Jericho? Absolutely not, nor were they allowed to make a deal with any of the peoples of Canaan! Did they have an attitude and a demeanor which provoked confrontation and war? One hundred percent! Were they personally allowed to take any spoil from the worldly goods of Jericho? Not even a penny! Were they required, while they were *driving them out* "little by little," to be the Old Testament version of salt and light? Of course they were! They were God's representatives on the earth.

Gradualism is not merely the concept of a *gradual* taking back of the culture and government from licentiousness and returning it to moral principle. In my opinion, the problem is threefold:

1) As seen from the example of the Jericho story, most of the *gradualists* seem to be very selective in the verses they use, such as Exodus 23:30. At the same time, they ignore the countless scriptures (i.e. verse 31) that show God's people carrying on an all-out battle, a one hundred percent confrontation. For example, they like to proclaim that Esther kept secret the fact that she was Jewish, and that the spies who searched out the Promised Land obviously did so in secret, thus justifying and supporting an overall policy of stealth. What they don't mention, however, is that eventually the same Israelites who sent the spies in were the Israelites who marched around Jericho. Nor do they acknowledge that the same Esther who kept her nationality quiet for a brief period took her life in her hands when she went in to reveal her identity fully to the king. When we compare all the times that Israel was open and public about who they were and what they stood for, to the few times that they engaged in covert activity such as sending twelve spies into the land, we see that the covert activity is the exception, not the rule. The rule is that we are to let our light shine publicly (see the discussion in chapter 5). The exceptions to the rule occur when a short-term situation, may justify a temporary withholding of our light or witness, but we do not substitute the exception for the day-to-day rule.

2) The problem, as previously stated, is a belief that in order to advance a righteous agenda we need to compromise righteousness in our voting and in other political decisions. This is an impossible concept since we reap what we sow. Romans 3:8 adds: "And why not say, 'Let us do evil that good may come'? — as we are slanderously reported and some affirm that we say. Their condemnation is just."

Though this scripture is referring to a distortion made of the Apostle's teaching (that "where sin abounds grace does much more abound"), the stated concept applies to what I am saying. *We cannot do evil and create good. To compromise and/or support the lesser of two evils is, in fact and in deed, an advancement of evil.* In the purely secular political realm, which is ruled by worldly concerns and priorities, compromise may be a pragmatic and acceptable choice; however, in the Kingdom of God, it advances the plans of those who are working against the purposes, will and holiness of God (the very enemies of His Christ).

3) Many gradualists believe in a concept known as Biblical Law. They believe in, and therefore desire to reinstitute, the Mosaic Law as civil law. The terms of this law include indentured slavery for those who can't pay their debts, capital punishment by stoning for certain offenses, and even a ban on wearing different fabrics at one time. Let me state that not all gradualists believe in the reestablishment of the Mosaic Law. Some accept varying degrees of the partial implementation of the Law of Moses as civil law. Others desire that every jot and tittle of the Law be in effect.

It is my opinion that these brothers in Christ are wrong at the very heart of the matter, which is that there are two different and distinct covenants, the *old* and the *new*. The differences go deeper than, but nevertheless include, the distinction between the blood of bulls or goats and the blood of Christ. There are critical differences between a written code and grace, between works and faith, between shadow and substance, between patterns and reality, and between guilt and forgiveness.

I believe that Romans 13 is the standard for government in this age. If the Holy Spirit specifically had wanted the Old Covenant Mosaic Law in its entirety to be reinstated as civil law, Romans 13 is the place where He could have and would have said so. It is likely that such a specific and important plan as instituting the entire Mosaic Law as civil law would have been expressed as a plainly-stated directive. But instead the Holy Spirit simply said that government was not to be "a terror to good works but to evil." The New Covenant commission on government, clearly stated in Romans 13, uses the most general terms possible. Now, this is not to say that much of the Old Covenant Law is not adaptable to present-day civil law. In fact, most of our civil law is derived from the Law of Moses. However, I take exception to the stated belief of the gradualists that God has directly commissioned the Church to implement every jot and tittle of the Law, or most of it. That law which relates to the *good and evil* referred to in Romans 13 has already been fairly successfully incorporated into our present day civil statutes.

Under the *gradualist* philosophy of stealth, fear, compromise and voting for the lesser evil, the reality of recent decades has been a *gradual* and consistent decline into immorality and paganism. It is a self-defeating philosophy because if the people we elect know we allow compromise, they also will compromise, and at critical times. Our philosophy has given them impunity, because we have told them by our voting that we will support evil as long as it is less evil than a stronger form of the same evil. **The old axiom *"Politics is the art of compromise"* is a statement made by and for compromisers — it is not for people who represent salt and light.** *Salt and light cannot compromise themselves.*

The only acceptable gradual approach to taking back moral ground is to take back, little by little, as much as we can, accepting partial success only as long as it is understood that all of the *promised land* is our inheritance. It should be the aim of salt and light to both defend and implement all the moral principles that God requires. Today we take Jericho; tomorrow we move on. But never is it proper to vote for a piece of legislation that gives up any moral territory we already possess or to vote for a candidate who will work to advance unrighteousness. There may be valid reasons to vote for one good candidate over another good candidate, but never is it acceptable to reject a candidate who stands for right principles in favor of one who does not — politics cannot supersede moral principle. Whatever the dilemma you face when you are voting, it is better to write in the name of someone who represents your values than to vote for someone who may, in fact, be an agent for the enemies of Christ. Let us look again at II Corinthians 11:13-15:

> For such are false apostles, deceitful workers, transforming themselves into apostles of Christ. And no wonder! For Satan himself transforms himself into an angel of light. Therefore it is no great thing if *his ministers* also transform themselves into ministers of righteousness, whose end will be according to their works.

Remember that civil officials are given by the Holy Spirit the title of "ministers of God" (Romans 13:4). Do you think it is highly likely that satan has his ministers in the political arena as well? Of course he does! Let me say it again — of course satan has "his ministers" in the political arena. And it is sad and shameful that many believers regularly vote for them. Let us also look again at I Timothy 4:1-3, which says:

> Now the Spirit expressly says that in latter times some will depart from the faith, giving heed to deceiving spirits and doctrines of demons, speaking lies in hypocrisy, having their own conscience seared with a hot iron, forbidding to marry, and commanding to abstain from foods which God created to be received with thanksgiving by those who believe and know the truth.

Note that the individuals who will get seduced by these demons will also "forbid" or "command" others to not eat meat or enter into the institution of marriage. This is a strong indication that these doctrines will also become public policy. And if these teachings against eating meat and against marriage come from demons, who or what is behind the teachings and public policy on the subjects of abortion, assisted suicide, pornography and homosexuality? When all else is stripped away, this battle is being fought between good and evil, between God and satan. If this is so, how can believers support candidates who support policies that come from demons? Yet this is exactly what has been happening, and it has been encouraged for several decades by leaders who should know better.

Thus, we will never make progress in restoring the moral foundation of our culture until all of God's people stop the practice of supporting the enemies of Christ. We will restore our moral culture only when we recognize that God is sovereign over the governmental affairs of man. And He is undeniably politically involved. With Him He brings His moral standards and principles. Therefore, the foremost rule is that we, His people, are to conform to His purposes, will and divine nature, yielding to the ownership of Christ — even in the political arena.

Once this rule is established in each of our lives, of next major import is that we realize that we are God's system of checks and balances for the strong worldly influences in our communities. We are responsible, as salt and light, for city hall, our county commission and our school board. Elected officials of such institutions are using our God's authority. What are they doing with it? Whose *ministers* are running our schools? Whose *ministers* have we elected to our state government? Whose *ministers* have we sent to Washington, D.C.? If they are not carrying out God's mandate for "His ministers," which is to encourage good and fight against evil in our culture, they must be replaced. They must be voted (*driven*) out.

Focus your energy by joining with like-minded people. There are many good organizations out there. Some of them are listed in the back of this book. If we are going to see restoration, then we each have a portion of the wall to rebuild. And following the pattern of Moses, who organized the people under captains of tens, hundreds and thousands, each of you needs to become a local leader in one of these organizations (a captain) and to take responsibility for your section of the wall. Support the restoration with both your time and finances.

Not everyone is called to run for elected office, but if God calls you to do so (pastors and elders, some in your congregation have the call of God on their lives to do just that; you need to encourage and support them), be not only willing but also be determined not to compromise. Be salt and light. Be fully and completely *God's minister* in the public arena.

Let each and every one of us become a source and channel of information. When you read a good article or book that is relevant to the culture war, pass it on. Or when you run across an interesting and important news story, photocopy it and send it out to your section of the wall and beyond. At the very least, keep your friends and relatives informed. If your local newspaper writes a slanted, biased story or editorial, respond to it as follows:

  1) Write a letter to the editor;
  2) Call the person who wrote the story
    and complain;
  3) If the paper does not respond in a fair manner,
    begin to contact the advertisers;
  4) As a last resort, cancel your subscription,
    and tell them why.

Remember, we are in a culture war, a battle between good and evil. We must approach it as such. We must challenge wrongdoing, even if we see it in the media. This includes radio, television, magazines and newspapers.

You need to become informed about which companies and businesses are funding the moral degeneration of our society. Then become pro-active by **1)** refusing to buy their products or use their services and **2)** placing a phone call to tell them why. Up-to-date information on all this can be obtained from the American Family Association (AFA) — see Appendix B in the back of the book. Also support the AFA financially for the continuance and expansion of this much-needed ministry.

To restore moral standards to our culture, we must take this war seriously. It would seem that a logical and sensible first step is that each one of us should purpose in ourselves to refuse to vote for the enemy or to fund his business efforts. Unless we stop aiding and abetting those who are working to increase the darkness, the end result will be the enslavement of many more souls to the prince of darkness for eternity. We are then no better than traitors to the Throne of Heaven, as well as a disgrace to the thousands who have given their very lives for the faith.

Along the same lines, decide to patronize businesses and companies that support the restoration of moral values. The liberal left understands and has long implemented this policy — except that they do so against righteousness and against God's moral principles.

Anyone who believes in the One True God is obligated to be an active participant in the battle. At a bare minimum, we should not be supporting the enemy. In truth, we should be like our Founding Fathers, but there are so few, who, as they did in the Declaration of Independence, have pledged to each other their lives, fortunes and sacred honor. Today, most Americans are unwilling to even pledge their TV time, let alone their lives. Today *the many* are not even willing to pledge the money they spend on vacations, hobbies, sports or other pleasures, let alone their entire fortunes. Today, the vast majority are unwilling even to pledge to publicly support righteousness for fear of being called names, let alone to pledge their sacred honor. Today, *the many* would not endure the hardship of missing a trip to McDonald's, let alone endure a winter at Valley Forge without proper clothing and supplies.

This lack of courage and obedience on the part of God's people is the primary cause for the moral deterioration in our country. If His representatives on this earth were both obedient and courageous, evil would be restrained. The fact that the darkness has been growing during this present time period (during our watch on the wall, when we are responsible before God to be the salt and light to this world) is proof positive, recorded on the canvas of reality which is God Himself, that you and I have not been doing our duty. When the darkness increases, someone is turning down the light. Where darkness is decreasing, someone is turning up the light. No matter what the outcome or the price to be paid (consider the price John the Baptist paid at the hands of Herod or the one the Apostle Paul paid at the hands of Nero), we are never to turn down the light.

It is clear God wants certain actions from us in regard to our culture, nation and other governments of the world. God wants us to be His ambassadors to this world, not only to represent His saving grace, but also, and equally as important, to represent His righteousness to the world. There is no escape from this divine responsibility to be involved, except in rebellion against the Kingdom of Heaven.

How do we then approach this requirement? Just as we would any other Christian responsibility — yielding to the empowering of the Holy Spirit to accomplish it. "To him that knows to do good and does not do it, to him it is sin." (James 4:17). What goes on in any culture, government or nation is of great concern to God. If the nation implements policies and actions that are in defiance to God's moral standards, He will move toward national judgment — unless, as happened in Nineveh, there is community-wide repentance.

As we have been seeing, there must be a representation, an involvement, God's people reflecting God's will and desires to the nation. This was symbolized in Jonah, reluctant as he was. But as Jonah fled to Tarshish, so today, many Christians are fleeing from their responsibility to their nation and culture. Jonah 1:1-2 says:

> Now the word of the Lord came to Jonah the son of Amittai, saying, *"Arise, go to Nineveh,* that great city, and cry out against it; for their wickedness has come up before Me."

Again, it is clear to see that God is greatly concerned with the wickedness of any community, even Nineveh, even your community, because all is under His authority and within His jurisdiction. Being salt and light to the world is to be a "Jonah" to our present-day Nineveh's. There are two questions that remain: Has "the word of the Lord" come to you as it came to Jonah? Matthew 5:13-16 is "the word of the Lord" to you:

> You are the salt of the earth; but if the salt loses its flavor, how shall it be seasoned? It is then good for nothing but to be thrown out and trampled underfoot by men. You are the light of the world. A city that is set on a hill cannot be hidden. Nor do they light a lamp and put it under a basket, but on a lampstand, and it gives light to all who are in the house. Let your light so shine before men, that they may see your good works and glorify your Father in heaven.

Therefore the word of the Lord has come to you. The second question is: In which of the two directions are you headed? Are you headed toward Nineveh or Tarshish? If you are headed toward Tarshish, then just as Jonah, you are acting in rebellion to God. If you are headed toward Nineveh, desiring to do God's will, then let us get serious about the Lord's call and manifest the full measure required by the words salt and light. Let us have our heart, mind and spirit transformed so that we will fulfill the "word of the Lord" toward us.

As we walk in obedience to God's call, perhaps what happened in Nineveh will also happen in our nation or community. Jonah 3:4-10 reads:

> And Jonah began to enter the city on the first day's walk. Then he cried out and said, "Yet forty days, and Nineveh shall be overthrown!" So the people of Nineveh believed God, proclaimed a fast, and put on sackcloth, from the greatest to the least of them. Then word came to the king of Nineveh; and he arose from his throne and laid aside his robe, covered himself with sackcloth and sat in ashes. And he caused it to be proclaimed and published throughout Nineveh by the decree of the king and his nobles, saying, "Let neither man nor beast, herd nor flock, taste anything; do not let them eat, or drink water. But let man and beast be covered with

sackcloth, and cry mightily to God; yes, let everyone turn from his evil way and from the violence that is in his hands. Who can tell if God will turn and relent, and turn away from His fierce anger, so that we may not perish?" Then God saw their works, that they turned from their evil way; and God relented from the disaster that He had said He would bring upon them, and He did not do it.

Notice that the repentance not only touched the community and the culture in Nineveh, but it also affected politics and government. For even the king physically humbled himself before God. He and the nobles then *legislated morality* and promoted religion through the state by putting out a decree that every citizen should repent, go on a fast, and turn from evil and violence. All this was done through the agency of the state. (A concept to the contrary is only in the mind of the godless or those who, for whatever reason, are allowing themselves to be influenced by them.)

To witness the same results in our nation in this present day, we who claim to be His people must, from our hearts and with seriousness of mind, show forth the attributes of being salt and light. If those attributes are of the quality that God desires, they will manifest themselves consistently on a day-to-day basis; they are compatible with, and thus will accompany, a renewed and submitted mind. God wants His people to be the salt and light of this world; therefore, part of being a Christian is to manifest these attributes — as God is involved so will His people be involved. If we want to change our culture, government or nation, as God did Nineveh, we can do it — if we really want to — if we become serious minded about that call on our lives — if we, in obedience, *arise and go to Nineveh.*

Colossians 3:1-3 says:

If then you were raised with Christ, seek those things which are above, where Christ is, sitting at the right hand of God. Set your mind on things above, not on things on the earth. For you died, and your life is hidden with Christ in God.

The transformation that must occur in our hearts and minds — "If then you were raised with Christ..." — is to be one where we are "filled with all the fullness of God" (Ephesians 3:19). The life we live while in this physical realm is to be one based on obedience to Kingdom authority.

As God is politically involved, so also will He lead us to be politically involved and to take a public stand for righteousness — if indeed we are willing to be filled with His fullness.

Chapter 9

The Goodness and Severity of God

The King James Bible translates Romans 11:22 as follows:

> Behold therefore the goodness and severity of God: on them which fell, severity; but toward thee, goodness, if thou continue in His goodness: otherwise thou also shalt be cut off.

The New King James says, "Therefore consider the goodness and severity of God...." The New International Version states, "Consider therefore the kindness and sternness of God...." J.B. Phillip translates, "You must try to appreciate both the kindness and the strict justice of God...." The New Living translation, "Notice how God is both kind and severe...."

Although I have stated it several times and in various ways throughout the pages of this book, it is needful to reiterate that God is neither exclusively merciful nor exclusively severe. He is both, equally and simultaneously, as we see clearly in Romans 11:22. The severity of God and His goodness are equally expressions of God's divine nature. It is the carnal nature (the sinful nature that we received after Adam's fall) that attempts to diminish this reality. For there are those who think that a God who can be stern and severe in exercising strict justice is unbecoming to their modern, progressive and sophisticated form of religion. Such a notion is humanistic — even demonic — and should be treated as such, summarily rejected and dismissed. For God is who He is and He will not alter His holiness or moral purity for anyone, even if such a notion were possible. In fact, all must and will conform to His righteous nature. Those who refuse to comply will experience severity, sternness and strict justice. But toward those who acknowledge and accept His sovereignty and His covering of forgiveness in Christ Jesus (because we fall short of His glory), there is unbelievable kindness, mercy and goodness.

As God is capable of expressing both attributes, depending on the situation facing Him, so must we. For the last sentence in I John 4:17 says, "... because as *He is, so are we in this world.*" I Peter 1:4 says that we are "partakers of the *divine nature*" and Ephesians 3:19 adds; "... that *you* may be filled with *all* the *fullness of God.*" These scriptures leave no doubt that we are to manifest all of the great character traits of God Himself, not because of our own worthiness, but because of Christ. By His shed blood and through the work of the Cross, this great transformation takes place, and we become His representatives. There will be times in which we express His compassion with an overwhelming capacity to forgive and extend mercy and grace. Conversely, there will be situations in which we firmly oppose some challenge to God's righteousness, purpose or will, (as did Jesus with the money changers, or John the Baptist while confronting the religious leaders at the River Jordan or the Roman governor Herod, or the Apostle Paul in opposing idolatry at Ephesus).

The severity of God, His strict justice, has zero tolerance for open and defiant sin. For "[t]he way of the wicked is an abomination to the Lord...." (Proverbs 15:9). Ultimately, your sin is either covered by the blood of Christ, or it will condemn you to eternal separation from God, which is hell itself. If you have committed yourself to evil, you have God as an enemy and He has no problem saying it publicly. In fact, your ultimate judgment when God reveals all the hidden things, even the thoughts and intents of your heart, will be a public event. All will know. All excuses will be nullified. Justice and holiness demand this much; therefore, justice and holiness will have it. Jesus said in Luke 20:17-18:

> What then is this that is written: "The stone which the builders rejected has become the chief cornerstone?" Whoever falls on that stone will be bro-

ken; but on whomever it falls, will be ground to powder.

Behold the goodness and the severity of God. We are broken when we are convicted of our sin and repent before God, and His mercy receives us as though we had never sinned. We are ground to powder, however, when we refuse to repent, for He condemns us to eternal separation from Himself, according to His holy justice.

If the Church (His people) is the pillar of truth, filled with the fullness of God and partakers of the divine nature, will not His sternness be exhibited through us at times against some things? Of course it will — if He has access to and authority over our actions. And as we are obedient to Him, He will also display through us His goodness, evidenced in attitudes of compassion and mercy. If we are partaking of God's divine nature, we should be able to shift or flow as God Himself does, between these two basic characteristics, depending on the circumstances we are facing. We will pull down strongholds; we will visit the orphans and the widows in their trouble. We will cast down arguments; we will clothe the naked. We will cast down every high thing that exalts itself against the knowledge of God; we will minister to those in prison. We will bring every thought into obedience to Christ; we will give food and drink to those who are hungry and thirsty. We will be good soldiers of Jesus Christ — warring against darkness, pleasing Him who enlisted us; we will be all things to all men that we might win the many.

God both confronts and comforts. He both accepts and rejects. He both convicts and forgives. We cannot obtain forgiveness for our sins unless we first confess that we are sinning. Likewise, there is no acceptance by God unless one first acknowledges and submits to Him as God Almighty, the One True God. And without a doubt, He will reject everything and everyone who does not, from the heart, accept Him and walk in a manner that acknowledges His sovereignty. For at the heart of salvation is a submission to Him as God.

Foremost in this truth, we have seen that all authority in Heaven and earth has been given to, and placed into, His Son Jesus Christ. As individuals and corporately, as the body of Christ (the Church), we have also been placed into Christ. When we are obedient to

Him, we will manifest the fullness of God. This fullness includes both His goodness and His justice, in balance.

I have attempted throughout this book to keep the teachings on involvement and on Christian confrontation in proper balance, while at the same time presenting this doctrine as God gave it to me. This balance is maintained by adding these truths to all other Christian expressions that God requires when we yield to the divine nature. This means that even though we must confront the evils of our day, we are not to be vengeful, for Hebrews 10:30 says, *"Vengeance is Mine, I will repay, says the Lord...."* Neither the individual Christian nor the Church has been delegated the authority or the right to exercise vengeance.

Do not allow yourself to be deceived by anyone. The witness that God requires is a full and complete witness, affecting equally all major spheres of human life on earth; religious, domestic and civil. When you stand up for "righteousness sake," you do not destroy your chance to share Christ, even though some Christians would have you believe that. Indeed, you enhance it because your testimony will ring true. It is based on the divine premise that God is holy and that He has authority and jurisdiction over everything. It is as certain as it can be, from a human perspective, that a person who is seeking the saving grace of our Lord Jesus Christ will actually find it, if the *true* witness is being presented.

However, Matthew 7:21-23 indicates in a very sobering way that *many* who personally call Jesus "Lord," even while doing what most people would consider great and wonderful works, will be told that they cannot enter the Kingdom of Heaven because, as verse 21 points out, they were not doing God's will. Verse 23 indicates that their works were actually lawlessness. Look at how the New Living Translation phrases these three verses in Matthew 7:

> Not all people who sound religious are really godly. They may refer to me as "Lord," but they still won't enter the Kingdom of Heaven. The *decisive issue* is whether *they obey my Father* in heaven. On judgment day many will tell me, "Lord, Lord, we prophesied in your name and cast out demons in your

name and performed many miracles in your name." But I will reply, "I never knew you. Go away; the things you did were *unauthorized*."

All evildoing is a matter of unauthorized behavior. When we sin, it is an act of rebellion against the holy requirements of God's nature. Therefore, the "decisive issue" is always one of doing "the will of my Father in heaven," as Jesus said. Thus the "decisive issue" will always be one of authority: the authority of God Almighty versus the rebellion of man who wants to be independent of that authority. And as Jesus just said, if that question is not settled in a positive manner in our quest for salvation, He will declare to us, *"I never knew you; depart from Me, you who practice lawlessness!" (NKJ)*

When we witness, that is, give the message of salvation, our goal is to lead a person to sincerely and humbly repent of his sins, which were done contrary to and against the righteousness of God. The final act of repentance is the acceptance of the sacrifice that God offers in Christ Jesus. And if our salvation is sure, it will manifest itself in submission and obedience to His will. A Christian salvation experience that does not reestablish for a person God's authority over his life is incomplete at best; at worst it puts his soul in the category described in Matthew 7:21-23. For as we have established, the questions of authority and jurisdiction are the most important considerations with God. Because He is God, the Creator and source of all that exists, it will always be so. And because He is sovereign and His nature is moral perfection, His righteousness will always be the standard for all behavior.

Therefore, we must stand up for His holiness because it is the only acceptable standard there is, and because it is the very reason for our need for salvation. God is holy, so we need to be saved because we have fallen short of His glory.

It is essential, therefore, that we witness of His righteousness fully in a most open and public manner. Because of this righteousness we will be judged, and it is this righteousness that sent Jesus to secure our salvation. Again, let no one deceive you. It is impossible to give a true witness about the Messiah without witnessing about the authority and holiness of God. For Jesus Christ came to earth as the Lamb of God to sacrifice Himself as payment for the sins we committed against the very authority and holiness of God that some people, even some Christians, seem so intent on ignoring. This act of Christ cannot be separated from the reasons (violations against God's holiness) that prompted the act. When we attempt to do so, we create a threshold for salvation that does not exist. And that is the premise of Matthew 7:21-23.

If our life has been restored to obedience to the authority of God Almighty through the act of salvation, it will show in our conduct and priorities. Through the work which is initiated, maintained and completed in our salvation (i.e., the work of the cross, regeneration and sanctification), we are to put on the divine nature. In other words, we are to be transformed into the image of Jesus. This is accomplished by the Holy Spirit, living His holy life in and through us, and is the only way that we can live a life that is acceptable and pleasing to God. As this transformation occurs, we are to manifest the nature of God Himself. That is the will of God concerning each of us. And for the purposes of the teaching of this book, that transformation involves both the goodness and the strict justice of God.

As there is no conflict in God between these two great spiritual principles, there should be none in us. However, we are human, and therefore limited. We are in the very process of being transformed out of a condition of being "carnal, sold under sin." (Romans 7:14). That means we are more than capable of an unbalanced application of one principle or the other. When we are out of balance we are exhibiting unauthorized behavior, and thus not doing His will. We also fail to minister life to those outside of the covenant of grace. When we display *goodness* to a degree that diminishes *severity*, or when we manifest *severity* in a manner that minimizes *goodness*, we do not walk in the Light. When we are not being led by the Holy Spirit, we end up doing damage to the outworking of the purposes of God.

Overall, the Church as a whole has erred greatly on the side of *goodness*. When we emphasize the *goodness* of God in a manner that diminishes or excludes the role and application of His *justice*, then we have erred and our message has become a distortion. We can be assured that divine justice has not been lessened in God. Matthew 7:21-23 stands as a lighthouse on a rocky shore warning *many* that a day is fast approaching when *many* who say to Jesus "Lord, Lord" will, to their eternal detriment, face the reality that divine justice, authority and sovereignty do indeed exist as eternal absolutes in the character and nature of God.

Because of this overemphasis on God's *goodness* (in that it is not balanced with God's justice) in much of the Church, the presentation of the gospel has become distorted and the representation of the light has become skewed — so much so that courage and faith have been replaced with timidity and fear. The pulling down of strongholds has been replaced by the toleration of open and defiant sin. And worst of all, in many cases, is that the Church is offering the lost this distorted gospel, which may not be able to lead any soul to a saving knowledge of our Lord Jesus Christ.

Yet God is more than able to redeem the situation if the proper response to the convicting power of the Holy Spirit is made. First and foremost, it is necessary that His people be obedient to His will. In fact, *His people will be* obedient to His will as Matthew 7 indicates, for those who are not obedient, even while calling Him "Lord" with their words, are rejected. Faith without works is dead. Could this be what the Holy Spirit meant in II Corinthians 13:5? The Apostle wrote:

> Examine yourselves as to whether you are in the faith. Test yourselves. Do you not know yourselves, that Jesus Christ is in you? — unless indeed you are disqualified.

Obviously, at the close of this book, we cannot go into all the implications of this scripture, but suffice it to say there are those who think they are saved, but they are not. To avoid being in this position, you must make sure the following things are realities in your life:

1) That the person of Jesus Christ is actually in you (you are *born again* through the forgive-

ness of sins and by asking Jesus into your heart);
2) That He knows you and you know Him (fellowship is restored because the guilt is removed from the conscience);
3) That you have received the Holy Spirit (see Ephesians 1:13, I Corinthians 12:3 and Acts 19:2);
4) That you are doing His will (see Matthew 7:21, Hebrews 5:9, and I John 2:17).

If you have repented of your sins and these above-stated elements of salvation are in your life, then you can know most assuredly that you are, and will be, saved. If Jesus is in you, if you know Him and He knows you, if you have received the Holy Spirit and if you are obedient to His will, then depending on the circumstances and His leading, you will manifest both the goodness and the strict justice of God . You will do so because He is in you and you are obedient to His will.

The Holy Spirit will not allow you to become unbalanced if you are being obedient. The easiest way to determine if you are unbalanced is to analyze your response to either position. If you downplay or overemphasize either one, you are unbalanced in your representation of God's nature. It is proper in God through the Holy Spirit to challenge the imbalance wherever it resides. To overemphasize — or to attack — the love of God or His justice at the expense of one or the other is obviously not in accord with the divine nature, which equally manifests both love and justice. Love and justice are two interchangeable sides of the same coin; one is the heart of the other. Love is the guide of justice and justice is the guardian of love. Neither is divine without the other. For where there is justice without love there is no hope, and where there is love without justice there is no holiness. Both holiness and hope are eternal absolutes in God. There cannot, therefore, be any imbalance in God. If we are yielding to the divine nature through the influence of the Holy Spirit, we will be balanced in our presentation of His character.

We are on this earth to represent God, and not our own religious opinion about eternal things. Although each one of us is flawed and each one of us falls short, our commitment, nevertheless, is always to strive to please Him. If that is our commitment, the "working" that the Apostle talked about in Colossians 1:29 will also be at work in and through us. The Holy Spirit will purge from our thoughts and behavior all willingness to walk in apathy and fear. He will energize us to be involved in shining His light into all areas of human existence, because all areas of human existence are, at all times, answerable and accountable to God. Both the physical realm and the spiritual realm are under His authority.

It is the duty of every person who has recognized God's sovereignty — especially those who have accepted the sacrifice and lordship of His Christ — to first represent His moral sovereignty over all things to all people in all arenas of life. His Church, likewise, is to present His solution, which is the personal acceptance of the sacrifice of His Son on the cross.

After we have come to recognize that God requires us to be involved, we must let the Holy Spirit build in us the resolve to do His will, faithfully and consistently, in order to please Him. For God can clearly make known to us His purpose and will; He can redeem us from bondage; He can restore our soul; He can then give us His Holy Spirit to empower us. But if we still refuse to be obedient, we diminish the impact of His grace upon the culture. The moral standards around us will deteriorate, and human hearts will become darkened.

God has chosen to work through His people. As His people, therefore, we hold the key to the spiritual renewal and success of our nation at this time. We must yield to the Holy Spirit and do His will by standing up for "righteousness sake." The Church needs to gear up rapidly to meet the demands of this battle.

Spiritual leaders need to teach that God is politically involved, as are His people. They should teach that every Christian should be registered to vote and that they should vote only in submission to God's will and righteousness.

Some individuals will sense in their lives, the call of God to run for public office. Pastors should encourage (not discourage) those in their congregations who are called to become *God's ministers* in the public arena.

Each church fellowship should have a public policy committee that keeps everyone informed on the issues of the day, as well as on key legislative bills and votes.

The pulpits need to ring with the message of recruitment, enlisting God's people to fight for what is right in the battle between good and evil in our culture.

Seminaries need to adopt programs to train *God's ministers* to serve in the public arena in every area from the arts to the media to public office.

Laying aside apathy and fear, we must, with courage, rush to the sound of gunfire. Wherever there is a challenge to God's sovereignty and righteousness, His people should be there, representing God's will and authority. We are His ambassadors. We are the salt of the earth and the light of the world. We are His soldiers in this life. Jesus said in Mark 8:34-38 (from the Amplified Bible):

> ...If anyone intends to come after Me, let him deny himself [forget, ignore, disown, and lose sight of himself and his own interests] and take up his cross, and [joining Me as a disciple and siding with My party] follow with Me [continually, cleaving steadfastly to Me]. For whoever wants to save his ... life, will lose it ... and whoever gives up his life [which is lived only on earth] for my sake and the Gospel's will save it [his higher, spiritual life in the eternal kingdom of God]. For what does it profit a man to gain the whole world, and forfeit his life [in the eternal kingdom of God]? For what can a man give as an exchange (a compensation, a ransom, in return) for his ... life?... *For whoever is ashamed [here and now] of Me and My words in this adulterous (unfaithful) and [preeminently] sinful generation, of him will the Son of Man also be ashamed when He comes in the glory (splendor and majesty) of His Father with the holy angels.*

As this age comes to a close, let us endeavor to bring as much glory to His name as we can, according to His mighty working which works in us. Let us not be ashamed to be called by His name. Let us be submissive and obedient to His will. Our Father has given us so much in His Son. Let us, at the very least, stand up with boldness to represent who He is, His love and His goodness, as well as His justice and His most holy nature.

Appendix A

Christian Presuppositions of "Secular" Government
by Scott Lively

Thus far this book has demonstrated through Biblical exegesis (interpretation of Scripture) that God is deeply involved in human affairs, especially in the political sense. In this section we move from the scriptural context and the history of ancient nations to our own national experience. We will see that God is and has always been politically involved in this nation as well. This section is not simply a recitation of statements by our Founding Fathers which support the claim that America is (or was) a Christian nation. Such statements do not by themselves prove the case. This evidence can be and has been explained away by those hostile to Christianity (including certain Supreme Court Justices). Nor is this section merely an attack on the "wall of separation between Church and State" — that much-misunderstood Jeffersonian metaphor which sits at the center of religious debate in this country.

God truly is involved in America, but his involvement is at a much deeper level than what is implied by the mere leadership or participation of Christians in its founding (though it is well documented that these men intended to establish a "Christian nation" as will be discussed below). God's plan for America is rooted in the order of creation itself; it is an outworking of the Biblical principle of human equality, derived from the fact that man and woman were created in the image of God, and established as a religious doctrine by Jesus and His Apostles in the New Testament.

In antiquity, genuine universal equality was never assumed. Even Aristotle, arguably the greatest of the Greek philosophers (who collectively are considered to be among the greatest and most enlightened thinkers of the ancient world) concluded that, while equality should exist for some, other people are by nature slaves.[1] Only Jesus Christ and His followers expressly taught that all human beings are equal before God and have an equal opportunity to accept Him and be saved. As Paul said in Galatians (flaunting every social convention of his age), "There is neither Jew nor Greek, there is neither slave nor free, there is neither male nor female; for you are all one in Christ Jesus"[2] (NKJ).

Although disregarded for centuries in which first the Holy Roman Empire and then a series of "divine" monarchs maintained social class systems, the Christian doctrine of individual equality reemerged in the Protestant Reformation of the 16th century[3] and later became the centerpiece of "liberal" political philosophy during the Enlightenment (the "conservatives" of the day were the monarchists).[4] The doctrine of human equality made possible the development of "Natural Rights" theory, which, starting from the premise of equality, concluded that certain rights are self-evident and unalienable, such as the rights to life, liberty and property.[5] If these ideas sound familiar, it is for a good reason. These were the "political" theories which guided our Founding Fathers.[6] But these theories are much less "political" than they are theological. We will shortly explore this assertion and its ramifications more thoroughly but one additional point deserves mention here.

It is widely recognized that the political theories of the Founding Fathers were greatly influenced by the English political philosopher, John Locke. The primary source of ideas for American political theory was John Locke's *Two Treatises on Government*.[7] Interestingly, Locke's first treatise is in large part a defense of the Biblical origins of the concept of human equality, written to refute Sir Robert Filmer's claim that the Bible justifies the Divine Right of Kings (and that all others are born into servitude to one human monarch).[8] Locke wrote his second treatise as an application of the concept of human equality to the social contract theory of government (which, until this time, was also used to justify the monarchy).[9] Locke's second treatise was used by Thomas Jefferson as a model for our Declaration of Independence and its conclusions provided the greater part of the philosophical foundations for our Constitution.[10]

Locke is commonly labeled a Deist by modern secularists to distinguish him from Theists and thus supposedly to discredit the notion that Locke's ideas and inspiration were Christian.[11] This is nonsense, since Deism was as thoroughly Christian a belief system as Theism to the extent that either relates to the religious issues of today. Simply, the divide between Deists and Theists involved the question of God's supernatural intervention in human affairs (i.e. miracles). Deism, which was a very short-lived departure from Christian orthodoxy, argued that God does not intervene supernaturally.[12] Theism insists that He does.[13] Both schools held most other Christian doctrines in common, including particularly the belief that the God of the Bible created the universe according to His will and design, and that this design includes eternal physical and moral laws which bind all of creation.[14]

Locke, incidentally, was not a Deist, a fact which will be shown later in this section. However, for the sake of argument, let us assume that Locke and all of the Founding Fathers were Deists and that our government operates from Deistic and not Theistic premises. Would this discredit claims that America was established to be a "Christian" nation or that Christians have a duty to be politically involved? More importantly, can the political theory upon which America depends (whether Deistic or Theistic) successfully accommodate the conclusions which are being reached by modern secularists? Instinctively, Christians know that the answer to these questions is "no," but to defend this conclusion, or better, to persuade others to the truth, requires careful systematic reasoning.

The Importance of Presuppositions

In attempting to declare the Founders Deists, modern secularists tacitly admit that the philosophical presuppositions of our Founders truly matter. Even more significantly, their all-important doctrine of "separation of Church and State" depends entirely upon the evidence of such presuppositions in the legislative history of the First Amendment religion clauses: primarily Thomas Jefferson's "wall of separation" metaphor, taken from a private letter,[15] and James Madison's 1779 *Memorial and Remonstrance*, a fourteen point argument against a Virginia State Bill to pay for "Teachers of the Christian Religion" from public funds.[16] Both of these writings were cited prominently in the landmark 1947 Supreme Court decision, <u>Everson v. Board of Education of Ewing Township</u>.[17] <u>Everson</u> was the first case to list atheism with Christianity as equivalent religious beliefs toward which government must be neutral. This unprecedented judicial and legislative conception of "religious neutrality" has in turn resulted in subsequent civil laws and judicial decisions that every Christian recognizes as contrary to God's law and divine justice.[18] More importantly for the sake of persuading nonbelievers, these legal and judicial conclusions are incompatible with Jefferson's and Madison's own admittedly somewhat Deistic presuppositions and, thus, are internally logically indefensible.

Ironically, although their own position initially relied completely upon the evidence of legislative history, secularists today (including Supreme Court Justices) reject appeals to legislative history argued by traditionalists (i.e. the evidence that most of the Founding Fathers were orthodox Christians who consciously infused American government with the principles of Christianity).[19] While such hypocrisy is frustrating, our case does not necessarily depend upon proving the Founding Fathers were Christians. We can demonstrate that the principle which the secularists derived from their interpretation of legislative history — the principle of equality — itself (wholly apart from Jefferson's and Madison's views) rests upon Christian presuppositions which limit its application to law and public policy.

First, a word about logic. The elementary principles of logic are easy to understand. Every conclusion rests upon specific premises or presuppositions. If the premises are true, the conclusion will be sound (meaning logically necessary and not just accidentally correct).[20] In order to test one's conclusion, therefore, one must prove that his premises are true. Most people understand at least this much of the process of reason. Less understood is the fact that each premise is itself also a conclusion which rests upon yet more fundamental premises. These more fundamental premises are also conclusions which in turn rest upon yet more fundamental premises, like a stack of bricks, one upon another, leading all the way down to an original premise which itself is not dependent upon anything else. This original premise or presupposition is called the "prime reality" and is in an important sense always a religious belief because it represents a person's conception of the ultimate reality upon which all else depends.[21] A common term for the totality of this idea is "world view."

In the Christian world view, the preexistence of God is the prime reality. At the root of a Christian's conclusions or beliefs is a linear series of premises that begin with the assumption that God is the first cause by which all of reality can be explained.[22] Our belief in the efficacy of logic itself might be represented simplistically like this:

> 1) God created the universe: a vast material and spiritual reality which exists in perfect symbiosis reflecting a grand intelligent design.
> 2) God's design incorporates consistent fixed laws which are binding upon all creation.
> 3) God's law can be understood by a rational mind.
> 4) Human beings were created in the image of God and infused with rationality.
> 5) As a human being, I can know truth by thinking rationally.

Each of these conclusions depends for its validity upon its underlying premises, and would not be true without them.

While everyone can be said to hold a worldview, in practical terms no one but philosophers attempt to trace their beliefs to a prime reality, and even philosophers shortcut this process in daily living. Although some people are "deeper" thinkers than others, all of us accept certain conclusions to be true and no longer think to question the premises upon which they are founded. The authors refer to such a conclusion, when it is used as a basis for further conclusions, as an "assumed premise." (Most of us, appropriately so, share huge numbers of such assumed premises in common, e.g., the reliability of mathematics, the inevitability of death, the necessity of traffic laws). The problem with assumed premises, especially those that are less subject to immediate empirical proof, is that we sometimes forget what the premises were and, thus, we lose sight of our logical boundaries. As implied above, our conclusions have built-in logical boundaries because *every premise imposes preconditions upon any conclusions which are drawn from it* — they must conform to all prior conclusions along the trail of logic that begins with the prime reality. Another way to put it is that one cannot reach a valid conclusion which contradicts the premises of its premise.

Thinking in the abstract like this will seem foreign to many people at first, but intellectual mastery of these few basic insights is a key to finding (and explaining) the truth behind even the most rigorous controversies, and in doing so, proving the correctness of the Christian world view. This will be shown in our analysis of religious neutrality.

Having demonstrated the critical importance of presuppositions to any belief, it remains simply to be noted that this principle applies equally to the "beliefs" of government. One might in fact argue that presuppositions are qualitatively more important in relation to the beliefs of government, since 1) its decisions affect so many people, and 2) its size and complexity make its conclusions difficult to change.

Equality and Religious Neutrality

Next we will demonstrate the importance of equality as a political ideal and the failure of reason which attends its misapplication in the modern concept of religious neutrality. We will show that those who have been labeled as Deists, rather than denying Christianity, consciously and conspicuously embraced the Biblical presuppositions of the concept of equality, and that because of this their application of the principle produced valid conclusions about government and public policy. We will further show that the Founding Fathers, including especially Jefferson and Madison, also expressly and implicitly acknowledged the Biblical roots of equality and founded their conception of religious neutrality upon this principle. Finally, we will affirm that our Founders were unquestionably genuine Christian Theists and revisit what they had to say about America's relationship to God.

As noted above, the U. S. Supreme Court, misreading (or misrepresenting) the Founders' intentions, have (beginning with Everson) separated the principle of equality from its Biblical premises. The consequence of this in government and leading social institutions has been ever more glaring illogic in public policy and a concurrent gradual loss of moral authority in our leaders. Ironically, it was the desire for moral authority (on other than Biblical terms) which led to this separation by others in history. Misappropriation of the principle of equality as a moral premise has precedents in the theories of Utilitarianism and Marxism, which unintentionally provided the conceptual foundations of the governmental philosophies of Nazi Germany and Stalinist Russia respectively.

Seventeenth century Utilitarian theorist and atheist, Jeremy Bentham, adopted the principle of equality as an assumed premise for his moral standard of utility, in which avoidance of pain and pursuit of pleasure were the only determinants of right and wrong.[23] "The principle of utility," Bentham said, measures every action "according to the tendency ...to augment or diminish the happiness of the individual whose interest is in question" and defined "the interest of the community ... as the sum of the interests of the several members who compose it."[24] Thus, starting from the premise that human beings have inherent equality, but denying that they are limited by duties and moral restraints imposed by God, Bentham invented an alternative moral criterion to guide government: a vague "right" to happiness of which each citizen could demand an equal share. Without the moral boundaries inherent in the Biblical context, however, equality was quickly recognized as an arbitrary premise without the moral authority to deter the powerful from redefining utilitarianism to serve their own ends. The moral standard of Utility still ostensibly assumed the premise of equality, but vested the state with power to define "the greatest good for the greatest number" and thus became the political philosophy of choice for tyrants, including the fascists of the twentieth century.[25]

Likewise, Karl Marx forcefully rejected Christianity but appropriated its integral tenet of human equality as a moral prerequisite for economic justice. Marx's more elaborate theory, including the doctrine that human society is proceeding inexorably through an evolutionary process which will end in perfect economic communism, also resulted in totalitarianism. In contrast to the Biblical presuppositions of equality, which raise human individual worth and dignity to the highest level of social priority, Marxism subsumes individual rights beneath the needs of the collective, teaching that the end (an eventual egalitarian utopia) justifies the means (any tactics, even violent revolution, which will speed the process of social development toward the goal). Once again, the principle of equality remains the necessary assumed premise of the theory, but the conclusions drawn from the premise clearly contradict its inherent moral preconditions.

The Separation of State and Reason

For many years the United States government operated with full cognizance of the Biblical roots of its political philosophy. In the early 1800s, Justice Joseph Story wrote that when the Constitution and the First Amendment were adopted

> ...the general if not the universal sentiment in America was, that Christianity ought to receive encouragement from the state so far as it was not incompatible with the private rights of conscience and freedom of religious worship. An attempt to level all religions, and to make it a matter of state policy to hold all in utter indifference, would have created universal disapprobation, if not universal indignation.... The real object of the amendment was not to countenance, much less to advance, Mahomedanism, or Judaism, or infidelity, by prostrating Christianity; but to exclude all rivalry among Christian sects, and to prevent any national ecclesiastical establishment which should give to a hier-

archy the exclusive patronage of the national government.[26]

This sentiment was acknowledged in Supreme Court rulings for many years. Davis v. Beacon 133 U.S. 333 (1890) held that:

> The term "religion" has reference to one's views of his relations to his Creator, and to the obligations they impose of reverence for his being and character, and of obedience to his will.[27]

Distinctly Christian presuppositions are implied by the term "Creator" and the characterization of the Creator as a personal God who requires reverence and obedience. A more direct example is found in United States v. Macintosh 283 U.S. 605 (1931).

> We are a Christian people according to one another the equal right of religious freedom, and acknowledging with reverence the duty of obedience to the will of God.[28]

Yet more specific to the question is the language of the court in Zorach v Clauson 343 U.S. 306 (1952): "We are a religious people whose institutions presuppose a Supreme Being.[29] These assumptions are operative (but not specifically affirmed) in the landmark 1878 case of Reynolds v. United States 98 U.S. 145 in which a law prohibiting the Mormon practice of polygamy was held not to violate the Free Exercise Clause. We contend that the failure of the court to articulate and affirm its biblical assumptions in this case fostered confusion in the court's later approach to religion. This failure was critical in this case because its holding established the basis for deciding under which conditions government could Constitutionally regulate religion. Despite the failure of the Reynolds court to expressly affirm its biblical premises, one can be fairly confident from the context of the case (especially as it denounced polygamy in favor of monogamous marriage a cornerstone of Christian society) that such premises are implied. This implication can also be read from the courts discussion of Thomas Jefferson's views on religious freedom and the First Amendment. Chief Justice Waite, writing for the court, cited Jefferson:

> That to suffer the civil magistrate to intrude his powers into the field of opinion, and to restrain the profession or propagation of principles on supposition of their ill tendency, is a dangerous fallacy which at once destroys all religious liberty ... it is time enough for the rightful purposes of civil government for its officers to interfere when principles break out into overt acts against peace and good order.[30]

On this basis, the court ruled that "Congress was deprived of all legislative power over mere opinion, but was left free to reach actions which were in violation of social duties or were subversive of good order.[31] (This holding created what is known as the belief/action dichotomy: opinions are sacrosanct but actions can be regulated.) What is important to recognize here is the problem of moral authority for public policy that is presented by this holding vis-a-vis modern relativistic conceptions of secularism in government. In a Christian context, "social duties" and "good order" are reasonably simple to discern and/or legislate by reference to scripture, but how does a society order itself when it decides it must be religiously neutral at the philosophical level?

In order to hold that Christianity and atheism are equal for the purposes of achieving religious neutrality, one must assume that government can define and enforce equality on some basis other than that provided by the Biblical context. In essence the court has repeated the mistake of Bentham and Marx and believed that it can appropriate the principle of equality without honoring God's limitations and requirements. The result has been the institutionalization of moral relativism, which, if not reversed, can only result in serious social chaos. *Individual equality has been interpreted to mean equality of any beliefs which individuals might hold.* In practice this fallacy has already fostered great confusion in society:

"multiculturalism" is advanced as a social doctrine that teaches that all cultures are equal, yet Nazi skinheads and other unpopular groups are excluded on vague moral pretexts. The authors have no moral dillemma in excluding the beliefs of Nazi skinheads from social equality because we have the standard of Biblical morality to discern right from wrong. Those who have no such Biblical standard hypocritically assert confidently that "all truth is relative" but still manage to condemn those who disagree with them. We find a further example in the fact that impassioned social activists on issues such as abortion and "gay rights" display moral outrage on behalf of conduct which is blatantly immoral.

As we have maintained throughout this section, however, American political philosophy derives its moral authority from the principle of equality articulated by the Deists and Theists of the eighteenth century including, but not limited to our Founding Fathers.

Deism and Theism in American Political Philosophy

Secularists may dismiss arguments that our Founding Fathers were Christians on either 1) the assumption that the Founders were Deists, and that Deists were more like modern secularists than they were like their Theistic contemporaries, or 2) the belief that the Founders' Christian faith is irrelevant to the documents and institutions which they created. We will show that both of these positions are false. In doing so, we will demonstrate to the secularists the fact that their own logical presuppositions, to the extent that their beliefs incorporate the principle of equality, are actually Christian. Beginning with the statements of Thomas Jefferson and James Madison which were used to develop the doctrine of religious neutrality, we will work backward through history to examine the "pedigree" of the principle of equality.

We noted above that Jefferson was quoted by the <u>Reynolds</u> court as advocating a policy of strict noninterference with religious liberty unless it involved acts against "peace and good order." Superficially, Jefferson's apparent absolutism in denying government intrusion into the realm of religious opinion appears to support the idea of value-free religious pluralism, but Jefferson himself assumed a fairly narrow context (relative to the modern view of pluralism) for the ideas and opinions upon which government and public policy should be founded. In evidence of this, we note that in <u>Reynolds</u> the court also cited a segment of Jefferson's famous letter to the Danbury Baptist Association (in which he coined the phrase "wall of separation between Church and State") which instructs that the purpose of the First Amendment is to "restore man to all his natural rights, convinced he has no natural right in opposition to his social duties.[32] The concept of "natural rights" was an Enlightenment era derivation of natural law with pronounced Christian presuppositions.[33] Of the few specifically enumerated natural rights, the two foremost were individual freedom and equality.[34]

Of all the Founding Fathers, Thomas Jefferson's religious views were the closest to true deism. An overly simplistic explanation of deism compares its conception of God to be like a watchmaker and the Creation to be like a watch which He crafted, wound up, and then left alone to run by itself. Lost in this definition is the fact that even the most coldly pragmatic deists perceived themselves to be genuine Christians, fully accountable to Biblical commandments, and lived their lives accordingly. A passage from the Encyclopedia of the Enlightenment explains this:

> Deists, like many other committed Christians, were sensitive to the challenges to Christianity raised by the Scientific Revolution, by philosophical Skepticism, and by seventeenth-century Rationalism.... Deism tried to answer these questions and concerns by turning reason — the very source of threats to religious belief — into its major support. Most deists believed that reason and the related lawful, orderly, mathematical, rational universe presented by the Scientific Revolution actually testified to the existence of God. The very elegance and simplicity of the design of the universe proved that it had been created by a wise God, and the operation of the universe according to law ensured its morality, its basic goodness, and its benevolence ... Since

they viewed the universe as a rational place governed by laws instituted by God, deists tended to challenge aspects of Christianity that could not be explained by the laws of nature.[35]

Indeed, deism, though flawed in rejecting what it could not prove empirically, accurately reflected the Biblical view of reason and natural law, stated most clearly by the Apostle Paul in Romans 1:19-20:

> Because that which may be known of God is manifest in them, for God hath shewed it unto them. For the invisible things of him from the creation of the world are clearly seen, being understood by the things that are made, even his eternal power and Godhead; so that they are without excuse...

Yes, deism was wrong in denying miracles, but to the extent that theists of the eighteenth century rejected reason in favor of mysticism, they also deviated from genuine Biblical Christianity. Reason and faith work together in Christianity, not in opposition to each other.

In light of the above, we can recognize Thomas Jefferson's view of natural rights as decidedly Christian, even if we were to allow that it was entirely deistic. For example, the preamble to the "Virginia Bill for Religious Liberty" (attributed primarily to and originally written by Jefferson) asserts that "Almighty God hath created the mind free" ... and that He, "the Holy author of our religion, ...[is] Lord both of body and mind.[36] One can infer from this that Jefferson did not conceive of a government policy of religious neutrality which would question the sovereignty of the God of the Bible. It is also apparent that Jefferson viewed his efforts on behalf of religious freedom as being directed, not at leveling all possible religious opinions, but at most seeking to accommodate the monotheistic religions rooted in the Old Testament (Judaism, Christianity and Islam).

Yet Jefferson did not subscribe to the view of the Creator as a distant "watchmaker" God. His preamble to the Declaration of Independence, asserting "a firm reliance upon Divine Providence" and his insistence (engraved on the Jefferson Memorial) that "...liberties are the Gift of God ... not to be violated but with His wrath" indicate a belief in God's active and ongoing participation in human affairs.

Also influenced by deism was James Madison. Madison's *Memorial and Remonstrance* was considered at least as authoritative a source for the Supreme Court in defining religious neutrality as were Jefferson's writings. A review of this document will reveal Madison's undeniable Christian presuppositions. There follows a several excerpts from the relatively short essay which was written to oppose a Virginia State Assembly Bill entitled "A Bill establishing a provision for Teachers of the Christian Religion."

> 1. Because we hold it for a fundamental and undeniable truth, "that Religion or *the duty which we owe to our Creator* and the Manner of discharging it, can be directed only by reason and conviction, not by force or violence." The Religion then of every man must be left to the conviction and conscience of every man; and it is the right of every man to exercise it as these may dictate. This right is in its nature an unalienable right. It is unalienable; because the opinions of men, depending only on the evidence contemplated by their own minds, cannot follow the dictates of other men: it is unalienable also, because what is here a right towards men, is a duty towards the Creator. It is the duty of every man to render to the Creator such homage, and such only, as he believes to be acceptable to him. This duty is precedent both in order of time and degree of obligation, to the claims of Civil Society. *Before any man can be considered as a member of Civil Society, he must be considered as a subject of the Governor of the Universe. And if a member of Civil Society, who enteres into any*

subordinate Association, must always do it with a reservation of his duty to the general authority,; much more must every man who becomes a member of any Civil Society, do it with a saving of his allegiance to the Universal Sovereign... [emphasis ours].[37]

What is important to recognize in this passage is that Madison defines religious freedom as involving only the choice of how or whether one pays homage to God, the Creator of the Universe. He does not contemplate a definition of religion which denies the existence of God or which challenges His universal sovereignty or the jurisdiction of His laws over mankind. Such a jurisdiction is clearly implied in the word "unalienable." It is only because God's law rules all that men have rights and duties "precedent in ... time and degree of obligation, to the claims of Civil Society." What is equally significant for this study is the context in which Madison discusses equality. He opposed it:

> 4. Because, the bill violates that equality which ought to be the basis of every law... If "all men are by nature equally free and independent," all men are to be considered as entering into Society on equal conditions; as relinquishing no more, and therefore retaining no less, one than another, of their natural rights. Above all are they to be considered as retaining an "equal title to the free exercise of Religion according to the dictates of conscience." [38]

How would this bill violate equality? By denying an equal place for pagan religions? No. "The bill violates equality by subjecting some [Christian sects] to peculiar burdens ...[and] granting to others peculiar exemptions."[39] Tellingly, in this section Madison identifies Quakers and Menonites as separate "Religions" and in the next sentence, as "denominations" revealing that to him these words are synonymous.

As regards Madison's own religious convictions he makes quite clear his Christian motivations. In section 12, he opposed the bill:

> Because, the policy of the bill is adverse to the diffusion of the light of Christianity. The first wish of those who enjoy this precious gift, ought to be that it be imparted to the whole race of mankind...[The bill] discourages those who are strangers to the light of [revelation] from coming into the region of it; and countenances, by example the nations who continue in darkness, in shutting out those who might convey it to them. Instead of leveling as far as possible, every obstacle to the victorious progress of truth, the Bill with an ignoble and unchristian timidity would circumscribe it, with a wall of defense, against the encroachment of error.[40]

Lastly, we note Madison's personal conviction that the very success of the nation depended entirely upon preserving its Biblical presuppositions. "We have staked the whole future of American civilization," he said, "not upon the power of government, far from it. We have staked the future of all of our political institutions upon the capacity of each and all of us to govern ourselves according to the ten commandments of God."[41]

Before moving on, it is relevant to mention here that Jefferson's and Madison's views on the "separation of Church and State," (aside from the question of whether they were authentically Christian in their conception) were not adopted wholesale by the Constitutional Convention. As Justice Rehnquist observed in a dissenting opinion in <u>Wallace v. Jaffree</u>:

> "The House of Representatives took up the Northwest Ordinance [to govern the Northwest Territory] on the same day as Madison introduced his proposed amendments which became the Bill of Rights.... The Northwest Ordinance ... provided that "[r]eligion, morality and knowledge, being necessary to good government and the happiness of man-

kind, schools [including publicly funded Christian schools] and the means of education shall forever be encouraged."[42]

Justice Rehnquist further observed that the very delegates who approved the final wording of the First Amendment passed a resolution just a few days later calling upon President George Washington to issue a Thanksgiving Day Proclamation "offering an opportunity to all the citizens of the United States... [to give] Almighty God their sincere thanks for the many blessings he had poured down upon them."[43] The House specifically rejected the assertion by some of their number that the newly adopted First Amendment prohibited such a merging of government and religion. President Washington promptly assigned November 26th, 1789 to be a day "devoted by the people of these States to the service of that great and glorious Being who is the benefactor of all good that was, that is, or that will be ... the great Lord and Ruler of nations."[44] Justice Rehnquist expressly set forth these facts to "confirm the view that Congress did not mean that the government should be neutral between religion and irreligion."[45]

Having now demonstrated that neither Jefferson nor Madison can be honestly invoked by secularists to justify religious neutrality as they have defined it, we will now show that the principle of equality upon which these Founders based American political philosophy is also Christian in its origin. We turn to the Encyclopedia of the Enlightenment for insight into the history of equality as a political idea:

> Prior to the nineteenth century ... Christian dominated European societies were constructed according to hierarchical principles, which assigned people to functional groups and gave each group different privileges.... The notion of human equality received a major thrust forward during the Reformation when Protestants began asserting to varying degrees that all believing Christians have equal status. Protestants minimized and in some cases elimi-

nated, differences between the clergy and the laity. They stressed that all individuals could read the Bible and understand the truths of God without assistance from priests or ministers. This religious notion of human equality translated easily into political realms.... Rationalism and natural law provided the first impetus for modern notions of political equality ... [until John Locke's] idea of the social contract made basic human equality the foundation of all civil society.[46]

Here we find confirmation that equality was at once a religious and a political idea, rooted in the Bible and made applicable to government through reason.

John Locke is another indispensable contributor to American political philosophy who has been falsely labeled a deist by modern secularists. As a matter of fact, Locke wrote a lengthy treatise entitled *The Reasonableness of Christianity as Delivered in Scripture* in 1695 in opposition to deism, to demonstrate that faith and reason are not incompatible.[47] Locke's Christianity was not only genuinely theistic, it was the motivating force of his life. In a letter to the Bishop of Worcester, Locke wrote:

> The Holy Scripture is to me, and always will be, the constant guide of my assent; and I will always hearken to it, as containing the infallible truth relating to things of the highest concernment. And I wish I could say there are no mysteries in it; I acknowledge there are to me, and I fear always will be. But where I want the evidence of things, there yet is ground enough for me to believe, because God has said it; and I will presently condemn and quit any opinion of mine, as soon as I am shown that it is contrary to any revelation in the Holy Scripture.[48]

Did Locke divorce his private religious beliefs from his theory of government? Decidedly not. To the contrary, his theory derived from them. In his second treatise (which, again, was the model for our Declaration of Independence) Locke wrote that "Human Laws are measures in respect of Men whose Actions they must direct which Rules are two, the Law of God, and the Laws of Nature; so that *Laws Human must be made according the general Laws of Nature, and without any contradiction to any positive Law of Scripture, otherwise they are ill made* [emphasis ours].[49]

The point of the above is that the secularists' conception of religious neutrality, even when viewed in the light most favorable to their interpretation, does not comport with either the historical facts or their own implicit philosophical presuppositions. While the secularists' approach to religious neutrality gives the illusion of providing a comprehensive rational solution to the problem of ensuring religious freedom under the U.S. Constitution, it is a specious doctrine. As Locke remarked in his first treatise on government "Incoherencies in Matter, and Suppositions without Proofs put handsomely together in good Words and a plausible Style, are apt to pass for strong Reason and good Sense, til they come to be look'd into with Attention."[50]

Additional Documentary Evidence

Even the evidence which is marshalled by the secularists, when properly analyzed, proves our case for God's participation in the founding of this nation through the political activities of His people and through the power of the ideas that proceed from His Word. Our case is further strengthened when we look beyond the secularists' selective reading of the historic record. First, we find that every one of the foundational documents of our nation reflects a firm commitment to and reliance upon the God of the Bible. The Mayflower Compact of 1620 is our first great constitutional document. It is short enough to quote in its entirety:

> In the name of God, Amen. We whose names are underwritten, the loyal subjects of our dread sovereign Lord, King James, by the grace of God, of

> Great Britain, France, and Ireland king, defender of the faith, etc., having undertaken for the glory of God, and advancement of the Christian faith, and honor of our king and country, a voyage to plant the first colony in the Northern parts of Virginia, do by these presents solemnly and mutually in the presence of God, and of one another, covenant and combine ourselves together in a civil body politic, for our better ordering and preservation and furtherance the ends aforesaid; and by the virtue hereof to enact, constitute, and frame such just and equal laws, ordinances, acts, constitutions and offices, from time to time, as shall be thought most meet and convenient for the general good of all the colony, unto which we promise all due submission and obedience. In witness whereof we have hereunder subscribed our names at Cape Cod the 11th of November, in the year of the reign of our sovereign lord, King James, of England, France, and Ireland the eighteenth, and by Scotland the fifty fourth. Ano:Dom. 1620.[51]

In their own words the Pilgrims' purpose was "the glory of God and the advancement of the Christian faith."

America's first model Constitution, written for Connecticut in 1638 begins "For as much as it has pleased the almighty God by the wise disposition of his divine providence to so order and dispose of things" and continues with a listing of Constitutional provisions.[52]

The 1775 *Declaration of the Causes and Necessity of Taking Up Arms* concludes "With a humble confidence in the mercies of the supreme and impartial God and ruler of the universe, we most devoutly implore His divine goodness to protect us happily through this great conflict and to dispose our adversaries to reconciliation on reasonable terms, and thereby to relieve the empire from the calamities of war"[53]

The Declaration of Independence, as we know, is rich with statements and implications about the meaning and purpose of the Revolution and the values on which the nation is formed. It expressly enumerates "inalienable rights," established by "their Creator," "Nature's God" and concludes "with a firm reliance on the protection of divine providence."

Even the U.S. Constitution, intended merely to set forth the legal structure of American government, nevertheless reveals the Christian philosophy and perceptions of the Founding Founders in the often overlooked signature clause.

> Done in convention by the unanimous consent of the states present the seventeenth day of September in the year of our Lord one thousand seven hundred and eighty-seven and of the Independence of the United States of America the twelfth. IN witness whereof we have hereunto subscribed our names.

In this clause we find the formal acknowledgment of the lordship of Jesus Christ in the dating of the document. Moreover we discover that the Founders perceived the Declaration of Independence, with all of its bold theological and philosophical implications, as the actual founding document of the nation (it being signed twelve years before the Constitution).

Smiles of Heaven

God promises in scripture that he will bless those nations which worship Him. For example, Leviticus 26:3-9 says, "If you walk in My statutes and keep My commandment, and perform them I will look on you favorably and make you fruitful, multiply you and confirm My covenant with you" (NKJ). The Founding Fathers believed and relied upon these promises. As George Washington said in his First Inaugural Address:

> No people can be bound to acknowledge and adore the invisible hand which conducts the affairs of men more than the people of the United States. Every

step by which they have advanced to the character of an independent nation seems to have been distinguished by some token of providential agency We ought to be no less persuaded that the propitious smiles of heaven cannot be expected on a nation that disregards the eternal rules of order and right, which heaven itself has ordained.[54]

In The American Covenant, Marshall Foster and Elaine Swanson chronicle a number of miraculous events in American history which reveal the hand of God at work.

> The Pilgrims' unintentional landing in 1620 at Cape Cod was clearly providential. Instead of landing as planned in Virginia they were forced by weather conditions and dangerous shoals to land in Massachusetts. Their scouting parties discovered what is now Plymouth as the site of suitable habitation. "Had they arrived a few years earlier they would have been greeted by the fiercest tribes in the region, but in 1617 the Patuxet tribe which had occupied the area had been wiped out by a plague. It was perhaps the only place where they could have survived"[55]

The one survivor of the Patuxet tribe, named Squanto, played an important role in American history. Without him the Pilgrims might not have survived at all. Squanto, captured by a British Sea Captain in 1605 escaped in England where he learned the language. Later, employed as an interpreter by a Captain Dermer on a voyage to New England in 1618, Squanto "apparently jumped ship and headed for Plymouth" seeking his tribe:

> After searching in vain for survivors, he attached himself to the neighboring tribe of the Wampanoag. Fluent in English, he was led of God to offer his friendship and help to the Pilgrims when he learned

of their presence at Plymouth. He joined with them thereafter and converted to Christianity. Bradford says the he "was a special instrument sent of God for their good beyond their expectation." Without Squanto's help they might not have survived for he taught them how to plant corn, fertilizing it with fish. He also acted as their guide and, most important, was their interpreter in their dealings with the Wampanoag chief, Massasoit, in the crucial early days when it was vitally important for the Pilgrims to establish friendly relations with their Indian neighbors. With Squanto's aid as interpreter, a peace treaty that lasted 50 years was agreed upon, which treated both Indians and Pilgrims justly under the law. Through the hand of God, the Pilgrims did not share the fate of other English colonies in the New World which were wiped out by hostile Indians.[56]

Much later in history, specifically 1776, God's hand was again at work to preserve America. The British army under General Howe had pinned down George Washington's forces on Long Island. Surrounded on three sides by land troops and the British navy in the East River behind them it seemed like hope was lost. Then began Washington's desperate, bold strategy. He collected every vessel he could find from row boats to sloops and, manned by fishermen from Gloucester and Marblehead, he set out to evacuate his troops by night. A desperate measure, surely, and one surely doomed to failure. For would not the British see them in the moonlight or hear the splashing of their oars and the many sounds of 8,000 men being transported, however quiet they tried to be? But, as historian John Fiske writes: "The Americans had been remarkably favored by the sudden rise of a fog which covered the East River." In the morning the British discovered to their astonishment that their enemies had vanished even taking with them their provisions, horses and cannons! Fiske maintains that "So rare a chance of ending the war at a blow was never again to be offered to the British commanders."[57]

Our Obligation to be Politically Active

In previous chapters we have considered Romans Chapter 13 and the requirement that Christians be in subjection to governmental authority but are there special implications in this instruction for Americans? Romans 13:1-7 (NKJ) reads:

> Let every soul be subject to the governing authorities. For there is no authority except from God, and the authorities that exist are appointed by God. Therefore whoever resists the authority resists the ordinance of God, and those who resist will bring judgment on themselves. For rulers are not a terror to good works, but to evil. Do you want to be unafraid of the authority? Do what is good, and you will have praise for the same. For he is God's minister to you for good. But if you do evil, be afraid; for he does not bear the sword in vain; for he is God's minister, an avenger to execute wrath on him who practices evil. Therefore you must be subject, not only because of wrath but also for conscience' sake. For because of this you also pay taxes, for they are God's ministers attending continually to this very thing. Render therefore to all their due: taxes to whom taxes are due, customs to whom customs, fear to whom fear, honor to whom honor.

Throughout the centuries Christians have lived under various governmental authorities: theocratic heads of state, monarchs and dictators. The common characteristic of these governments was their sovereignty over the individual citizen. Government was not truly "by the consent of the governed" even after the rise of parliamentary systems following the Magna Carta. State authority and individual citizenship were distinct and separate spheres. Under these governments, therefore, Christian duty was limited to obedience to the state (subject, of course, to conscience and God's higher law per

Acts 4:18-20).

In American political theory, however, each individual enters society with an equal right (and, we would argue, duty) to influence government. No longer is a citizen powerless to make and enforce laws. In fact, such authority now rests entirely with the citizens. While government wields the sword, its power is derivative and not sovereign. The citizens hold power in common and delegate to government only so much authority as it needs to carry out its prescribed duties.

What does this imply for Christians? Since God instructs us that the purpose of government is to be a "terror to evil" and a "minister of good," and has given us individually the authority over government, aren't we then logically required to take an active role in political affairs? It would seem that these factors, considered in light of Christ's direct commandment to be "salt" and "light" to the world, compel Christians to actively participate in the American political process.

In conclusion, therefore, we see that God truly has been politically involved in America at every level: through the very laws of His creation upon which He caused us to found our national government, through the actions of His people, our Founding Fathers, and by direct supernatural intervention. What is most important, however, is that we realize that God's continuing blessings and preservation of America depend upon our faith and obedience, which we show by our individual *political* involvement. To the extent that we recognize the hand of God in our nation's history and the reality that our actions as a nation determine the nature of His continuing intervention, we should be motivated to exert our God-ordained moral authority to defend and to renew America's Christian heritage.

Appendix B

Organizations Active on Moral Issues

American Family Association (AFA)
107 Parkgate
PO Drawer 2440
Tupelo, MS 38803-9988
Legislative Lobby Office
227 Massachusetts Avenue NE, Suite 100A
Washington, DC 20070-1003
(601) 844-5036
(601) 844-9176 Fax
(202) 544-0061
(202) 544-0504 DC Fax
WWW: http://www.afa.net
Donald Wildmon, President

American Life League, Inc.
PO Box 1350
1179 Courthouse Rd.
Stafford, VA 22555
(540) 659-4171
(540) 659-2586 Fax
http://www.all.org
Judie Brown, President

Christian Coalition
PO Box 1990
1801-L Sara Drive
Chesapeake, VA 23327-1990
(800) 325-4746
(757) 424-2630
(757) 424-9068 Fax
WWW:http://www.infi.nct:80/cc/
Pat Robertson, Chairman
Don Hodel, President
Randy Tate, Executive Director

Christian Coalition (DC)
227 Massachusetts Avenue NE, Suite 101
Washington, DC 20002
(202) 547-3600
(202) 543-2978 Fax
Jeff Tayler, Government Relation Representative

Christian Women for America (DC)
1015 Fifteenth Street NW, Suite 1100
Washington, DC 20005
(202) 488-7000
(202) 488-0806 Fax
(800) 458-8797
Beverly LaHaye, Founder

Coral Ridge Ministries
PO Box 40
Ft. Lauderdale, FL 33302
(800) 229-9673
(954) 772-0404
(954) 491-7975 Fax
Dr. D. James Kennedy, Sr. Minister

Eagle Forum
Operations Center
PO Box 618
Alton, IL 62002
Capitol Hill Office:
316 Pennsylvania Ave SE
Washington, DC 20003
(618) 462-5415
(202) 544-0353 DC Office
eagle@eagleforum.org E-Mail
http://www.eagleforum.org
Phyllis Schlafly, President

Family Research Council
801 G Street NW
Washington, DC 20001
(800) 225-4008 Order Line
(202) 393-2134 Fax
www.frc.org
Gary Bauer, President

Focus on the Family
Colorado Springs, CO 80995
(719) 531-5181 General Questions
(719) 531-3424 Fax
(800) 232-6459 To Request Resources
www.family.org   E-Mail
Dr. James C. Dobson, President

Oregon Citizens Alliance
PO Box 9276
Brooks, OR 97305
(503) 463-0653
(503) 463-8745 Fax
bjmabon@aol.com   E-mail
Lon T. Mabon, Chairman

Right to Life Education Foundation, Inc.
PO Box 24073
Cincinnati, OH 45224
1802 W Galbraith Road
Cincinnati, OH 45239
(513) 729-4994 Fax
(513) 522-0820

Traditional Values Coalition (DC)
Washington Federal Affairs Office
139 C Street SE
Washington, DC 20003
(202) 547-8570
(202) 546-6403 Fax
Rev. Lou Sheldon, Chairman

Traditional Values Foundation/Coalition
100 S Anaheim Boulevard, Suite 350
Anaheim, CA 92805
PO Box 940
Anaheim, CA 92815-0940
(714) 520-0300
(202) 546-6403 DC Fax
(202) 547-8570 DC Office
Rev. Lou Sheldon, Chairman

Footnotes

Chapter 1
[1] Dictionary of Old Testament Words for English Readers by Aaron Pick.
[2] Old Testament Word Studies by William Wilson.
[3] Keil-Delitzsch, Commentary on the Old Testament.
[4] The Septuagint Version, With an English Translation by Charles Lee Brenton, Zondervan.
[5] *See* Keil-Delitzsch, *supra* note 3.

Chapter 2
[1] *A GREEK-ENGLISH LEXICON OF THE NEW TESTAMENT AND EARLY CHRISTIAN LITERATURE* by Bauer, Arndt, Gingrich, Pg. 18.

Chapter 3
[1] *See* Lexicon, *supra* Chapter 2, note 1 at page 238.

Appendix A
[1] DENNIS LLOYD, THE IDEA OF LAW 77 (1964).
[2] Galations 3:28 (New King James).
[3] PETER HANS REILL AND ELLEN JUDY WILSON, ENCYCLOPEDIA OF THE ENLIGHTENMENT 136 (1966)
[4] *Id.*
[5] *See Id.* at 301-302.
[6] *See generally* John Eidsmoe, *The Judeo-Christian Roots of the Constitution*, in RESTORING THE CONSTITUTION 1787-1987 (House, H. Wayne ed. 1987.)
[7] GARY T. AMOS, DEFENDING THE DECLARATION 2ff. (1989).
[8] JOHN LOCKE, TWO TREATISES OF GOVERNMENT (Peter Laslett ed., Cambridge University Press, 1980) (1690).
[9] *Id.*
[10] *See* Amos, *supra* note 7 at 2.

[11] *Id.* See 50-60.
[12] *See generally* Eidsmoe, *Supra* note 6.
[13] *Id.*
[14] *Id.*
[15] Reynolds v. United States, 98 U.S. 145, 164 (1878).
[16] *Id.* at 163.
[17] Everson v. Board of Education of Ewing Township, 330 U.S. 1
[18] William Stanmeyer, *Restoring the Faith of the Founders*, in RESTORING THE CONSTITUTION 1787-1987 27 (H. Wayne House ed., 1987).
[19] Lee v. Weisman, 505 U.S. 577, 610 (1992).
[20] RUGGERO J. ALDISERT, LOGIC FOR LAWYERS 3-11, 3-12 (1992).
[21] ROY A. CLOUSER, THE MYTH OF RELIGIOUS NEUTRALITY 22-23 (1991).
[22] JAMES W. SIRE, THE UNIVERSE NEXT DOOR 23-44 (1988).
[23] Jeremy Bentham, *An Introduction to the Principles of Morals and Legislation*, in THE GREAT LEGAL PHILOSOPHERS 262-263 (Clarence Morris ed., 1959).
[24] *See Id.* at 263.
[25] BRENDAN F. BROWN, THE NATURAL LAW READER 9 (1960).
[26] J. STORY, 2 COMMENTARIES ON THE CONSTITUTION OF THE UNITED STATES 593-95 (2nd ed. 1851).
[27] Davis v. Beacon 133 U.S. 333,342 (1890).
[28] United States v. Macintosh 283 U.S. 605, 625 (1931).
[29] Zorach v Clauson 343 U.S. 306, 313 (1952.
[30] Reynolds v. United States 98 U.S. 145, 163 (1878).
[31] *See Id.* at 164.
[32] *Id.*
[33] *See* Amos, *supra* note 7 at 103-126.
[34] *See* Reill, *supra* note 3 at 301-302.
[35] *Id.* at 106-107
[36] *See* Everson, supra note 17 at 12-13.
[37] James Madison, *Memorial and Remonstrance Against Religious Assessments*, in THE MIND OF THE FOUNDER 8-16 (Marvin Meyers ed., 1973).
[38] *Id.*
[39] *Id.*
[40] *Id.*
[41] DAVID BARTON, AMERICA'S GODLY HERITAGE 18 (1993).

[42] Wallace v. Jaffree 427 U.S.38, 100 (1985).
[43] *Id.*, at 101.
[44] *Id.*, at 102.
[45] *Id.*, at 100.
[46] *See* Reill, *supra* note 3 at 137-137.
[47] JOHN LOCKE, THE REASONABLENESS OF CHRISTIANITY (George W. Ewing ed., Regnery Gateway Inc. 1989) (1695).
[48] *Id.* at xi.
[49] WILLIAM J. FEDERER, AMERICA'S GOD AND COUNTRY 398 (1996).
[50] *See* Locke, *supra* note 8 at 173.
[51] *See* Federer, *supra* note 49 at 435-436.
[52] The American Covenant, Marshall Foster and Elaine Swanson 33.
[53] *Id.*
[54] *See* Federer, *supra* note 49 at 651-652.
[55] See Foster, supra note 52 at 38.
[56] *Id.* at 38f.
[57] *Id.* at 41.